# Stouffville Ontario Book 2 in Colour Photos, Saving Our History One Photo at a Time

Photography
by Barbara Raué
©2019

Series Name: Cruising Ontario

Book 222: Stouffville Book 2

Cover photo: 96 Church Street, Page 37

©All the photos in this book have been taken with my cameras. I own the rights to them.

# Series Name: Cruising Ontario
# Saving Our History One Photo at a Time
# in colour photos

Books Available in Alphabetical Order:
Aberfoyle, Acton, Ajax, Alton, Amherstburg, Ancaster, Arthur, Auburn, Aylmer, Ayr, Beaver Valley, Belgrave, Belleville, Bloomingdale, Blyth, Brantford, Brockville, Burford, Burlington, Caledon, Caledonia, Cambridge, Carlow, Chatsworth, Clifford, Collingwood, Conestogo, Delhi, Dorchester to Aylmer, Drayton, Drumbo, Dundas, Dunlop, Eden Mills, Elmira, Elora, Erin, Essex, Fergus, Goderich, Grimsby, Guelph, Hagersville, Hamilton, Hanover, Harriston, Hespeler, Jarvis, Kingston, Kingsville, Kitchener, Lake Superior, Lincoln, Linwood, Listowel, London, Lucknow, Merrickville, Mono, Mount Forest, Mount Pleasant, Neustadt, New Hamburg, Newboro, Newport, Niagara-on-the-Lake, Niagara Falls, North Bay, Oakville, Onondaga, Orangeville, Orillia, Oshawa, Owen Sound, Palmerston, Paris, Pelham, Perth, Peterborough, Petrolia, Pickering, Port Colborne, Port Elgin, Portland, Preston, Rockwood, Sarnia, Sault Ste. Marie, Seaforth, Sheffield, Shelburne, Simcoe, Smiths Falls, Smithville, Southampton, St. Catharines, St. George, St. Jacobs, St. Marys, St. Thomas, Stoney Creek, Stratford, Thamesford, Thunder Bay, Tillsonburg, Toronto, Waterdown, Waterford, Waterloo, Welland, Wellesley, West Flamborough, Westport, Whitby, Windsor, Wingham, Woodstock

Book 212-215 Haldimand County
Book 216: Sudbury
Book 217: Parry Sound
Book 218-219: Uxbridge
Book 220: Port Perry

Book 221-222: Stouffville

## Table of Contents

| | |
|---|---|
| Edward Street | Page 5 |
| Mill Street | Page 9 |
| O'Brien Avenue | Page 14 |
| Church Street | Page 29 |
| Frederick Street | Page 42 |
| George Street | Page 42 |
| Duchess Street | Page 44 |
| Victoria Street | Page 45 |
| Clarke Street | Page 53 |
| Somerville Street | Page 56 |
| Tenth Line | Page 57 |

On January 1, 1971, the Village of Stouffville amalgamated with Whitchurch Township and was designated a community within the larger town of Whitchurch-Stouffville, a municipality in the Greater Toronto Area, about fifty kilometers north of downtown Toronto. It is more than two hundred and six square kilometres in size, and located in the mid-eastern area of the Regional Municipality of York on the ecologically-sensitive Oak Ridges Moraine and the Rouge River watershed. Its motto since 1993 is "country close to the city".

Stouffville is the primary urban area within the town of Whitchurch-Stouffville. It is centred at the intersection of Main Street, Mill Street and Market Street. Stouffville was founded in 1804 by Abraham Stouffer who built a sawmill and grist-mill on the banks of Duffin's Creek in the 1820s.

Urban Stouffville stretches from the York-Durham Line to Highway 48 and is about 2.7 kilometers wide with development north and south of Main Street. Stouffville is bounded by farmland and a golf course. Uxbridge lies to the east.

Stouffville Station was built in 1871 by Toronto and Nipissing Railway connecting Stouffville and Uxbridge with Toronto. The line's north-eastern terminus at Coboconk, Ontario on Balsam Lake in the Kawarthas was completed in 1872. In 1877, a second track was built from Stouffville north to Jackson's Point on Lake Simcoe. These connections were to provide a reliable and efficient means of transporting timber harvested and milled in these regions. *Stouffville Junction* serviced thirty trains per day. The railway became the Grand Trunk Railway in 1884, and Canadian National Railways took over the line in 1914. Stouffville Station was demolished in 1980s and replaced by current GO station.

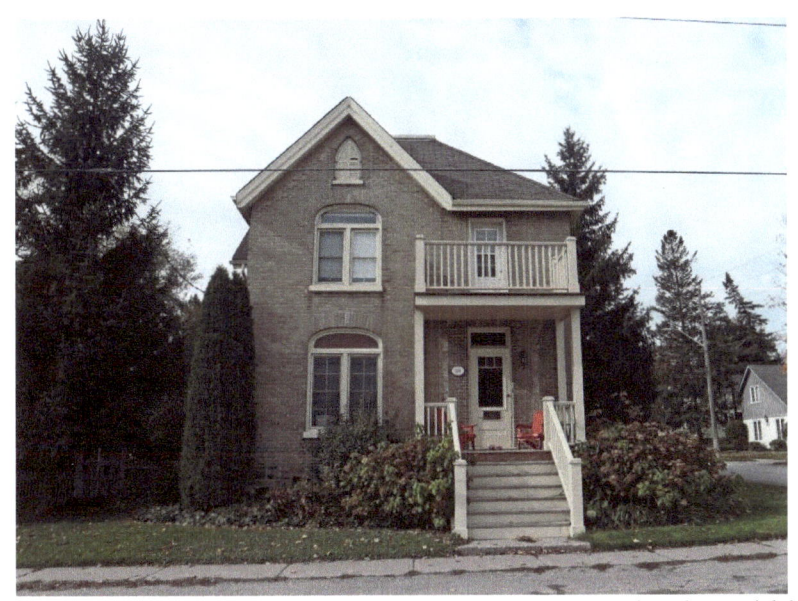

88 Edward Street – c. 1889 – Late Victorian Hybrid – rubble stone foundation, balcony over open porch

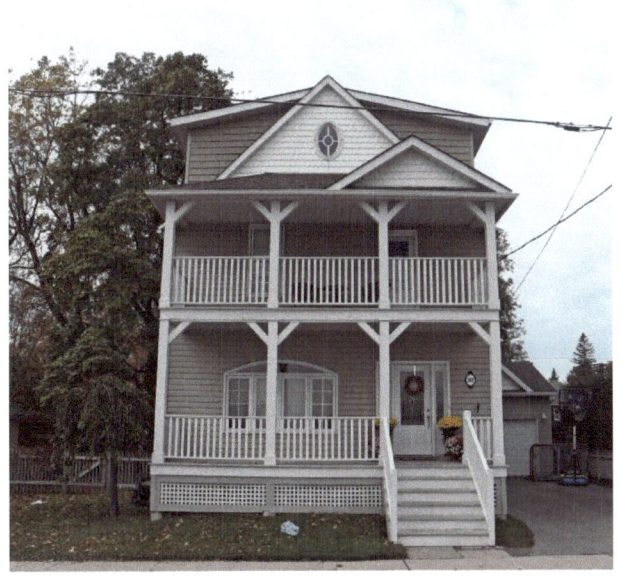

80 Edward Street – c. 1895

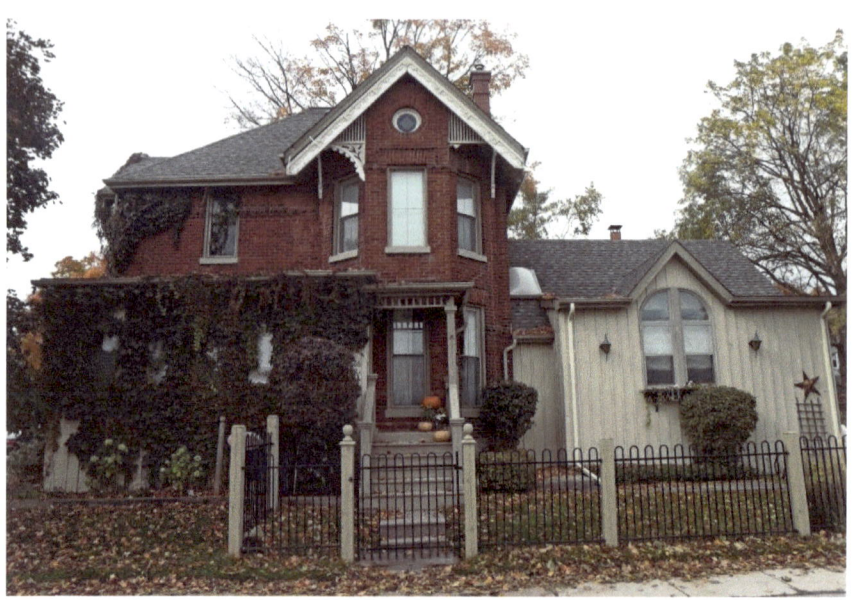

66 Edward Street – c. 1894 – Romanesque Revival - built by Nathan Forsyth for Louis Bartholomew – string course

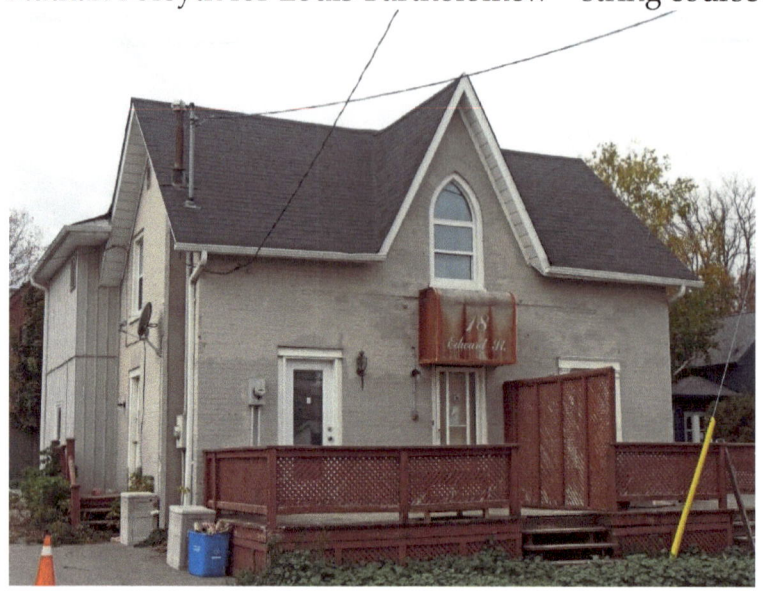

18 Edward Street – c. 1876 – Gothic Revival – original red brick painted over – first owner John McNeil, sawyer

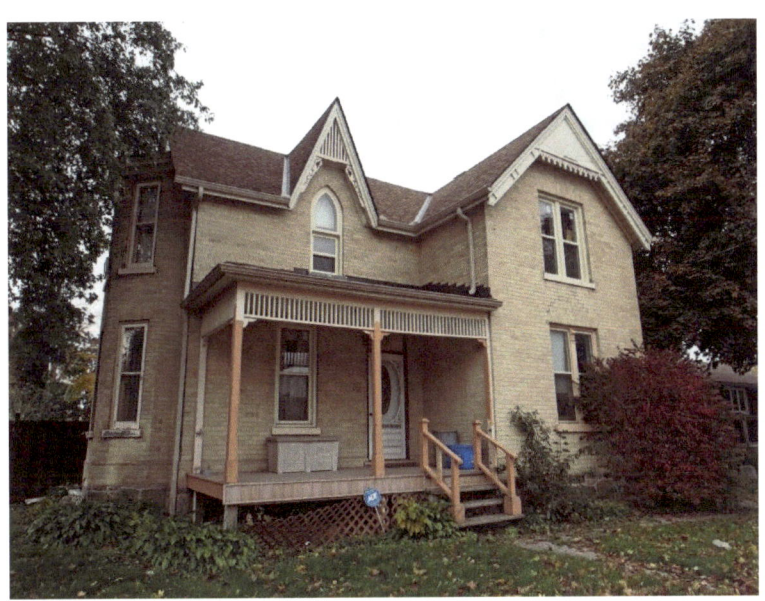

38 Edward Street – c. 1889 – Late Victorian Hybrid – starburst pediment design on larger gable – built by Peter Fleury, woodworker

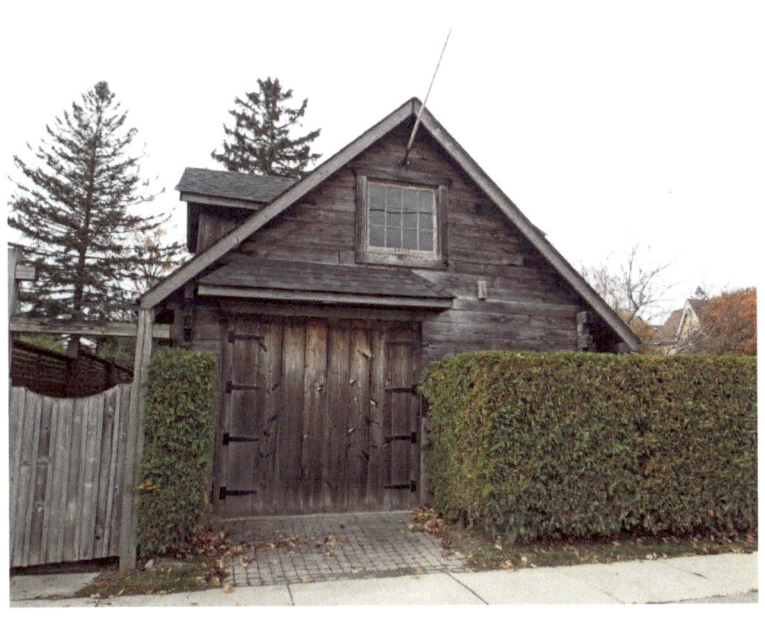

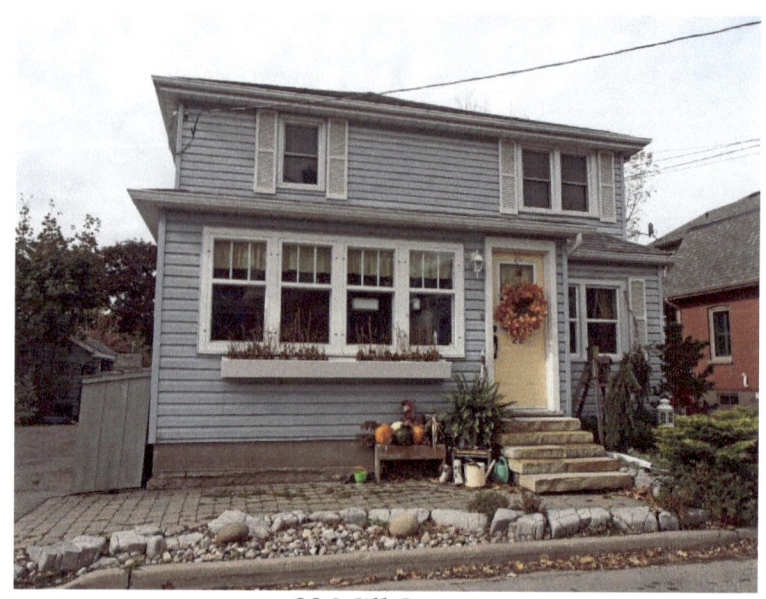

22 Mill Street

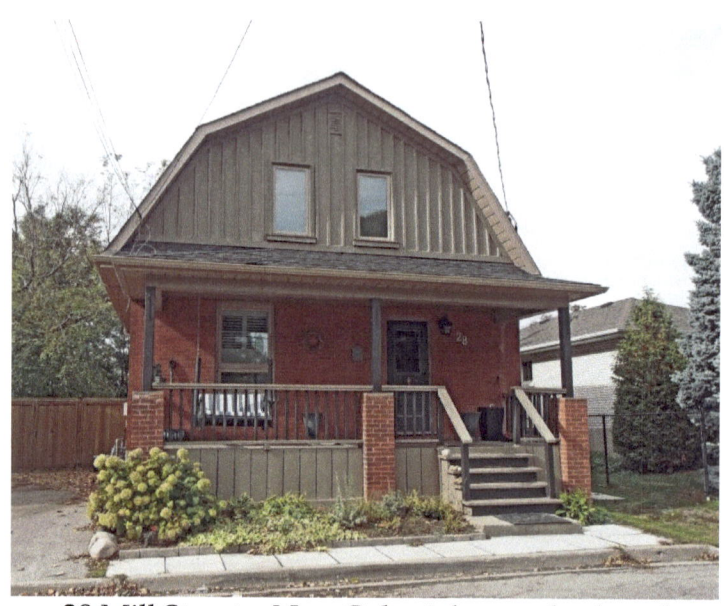

28 Mill Street – Neo-Colonial – gambrel roof

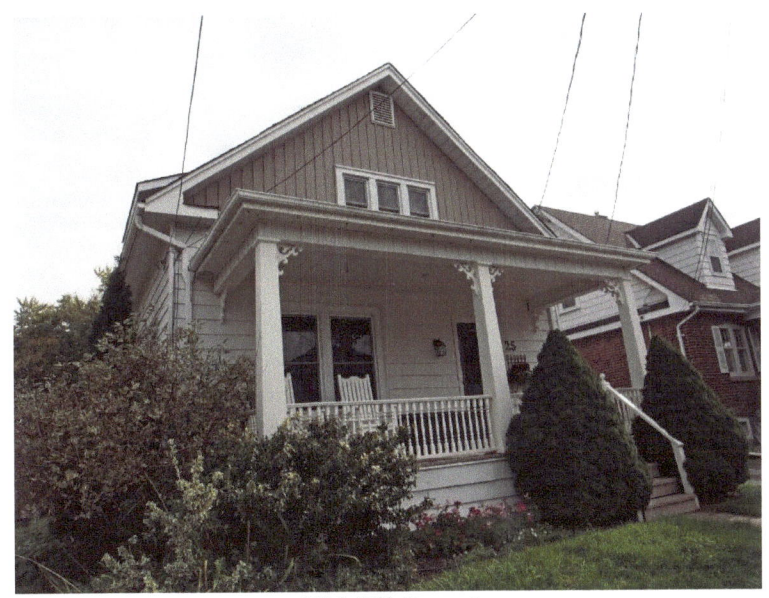

25 Mill Street

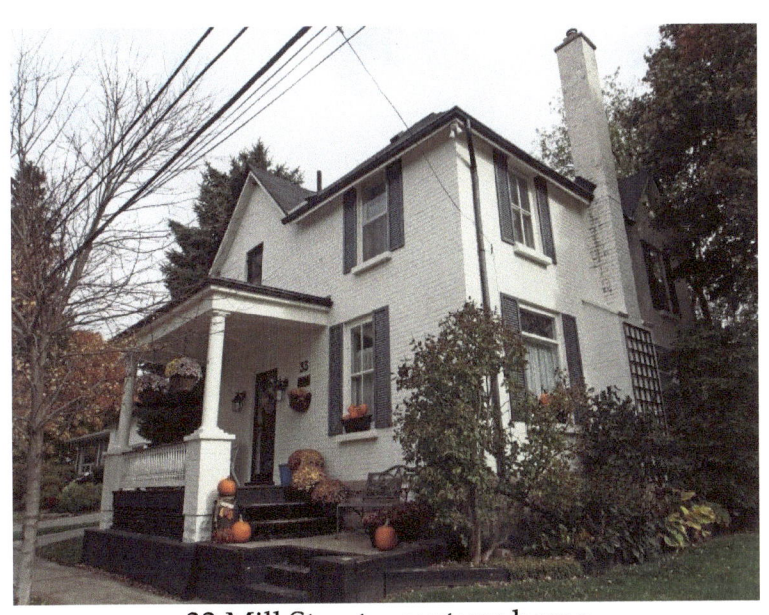

33 Mill Street – century home

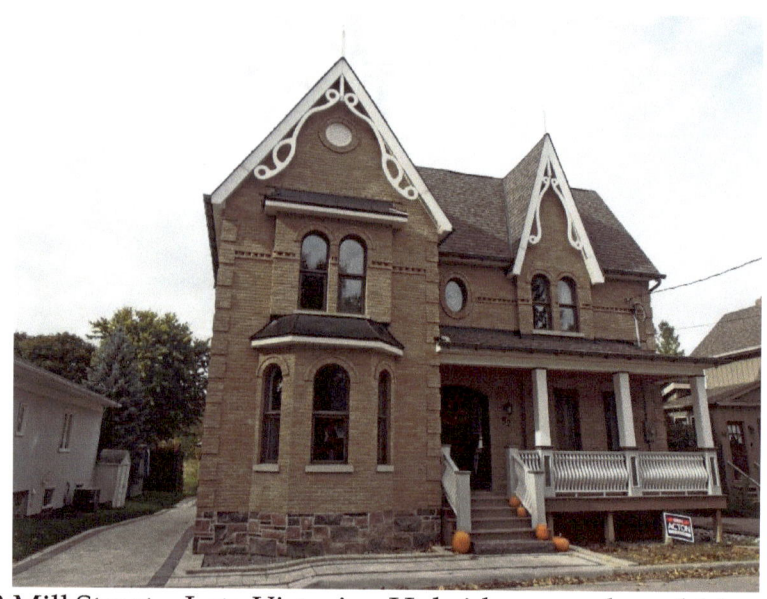

52 Mill Street – Late Victorian Hybrid – verge board trim on gables

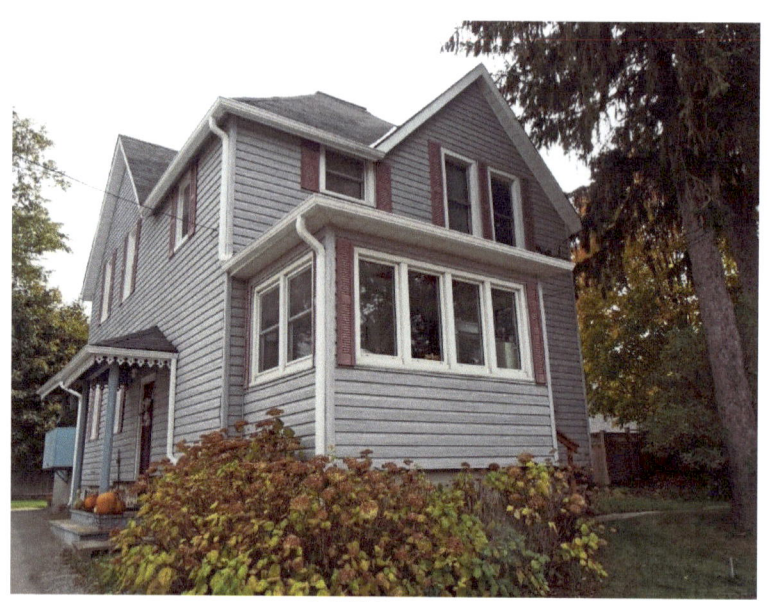

Mill Street

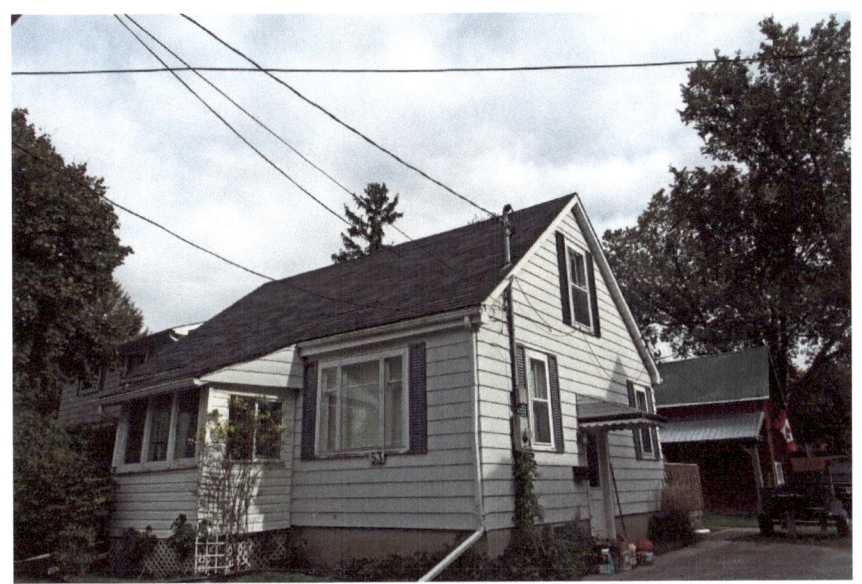

53 Mill Street

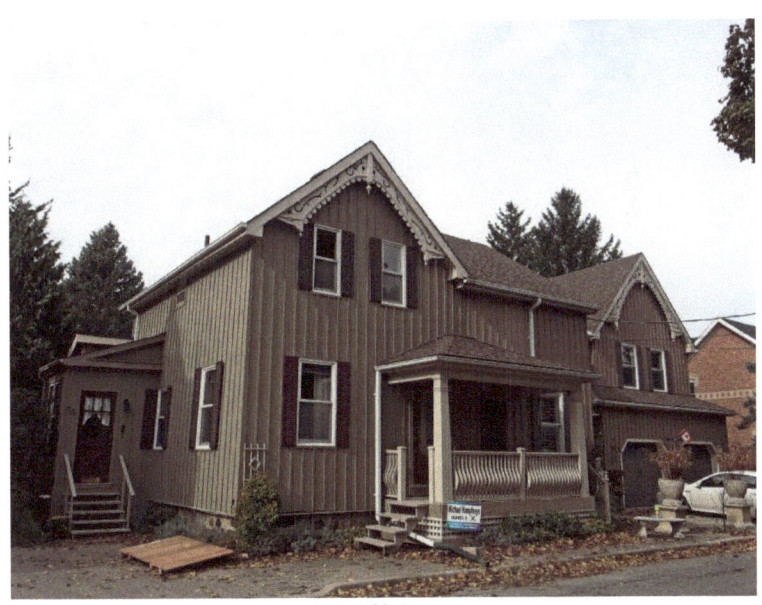

58 Mill Street

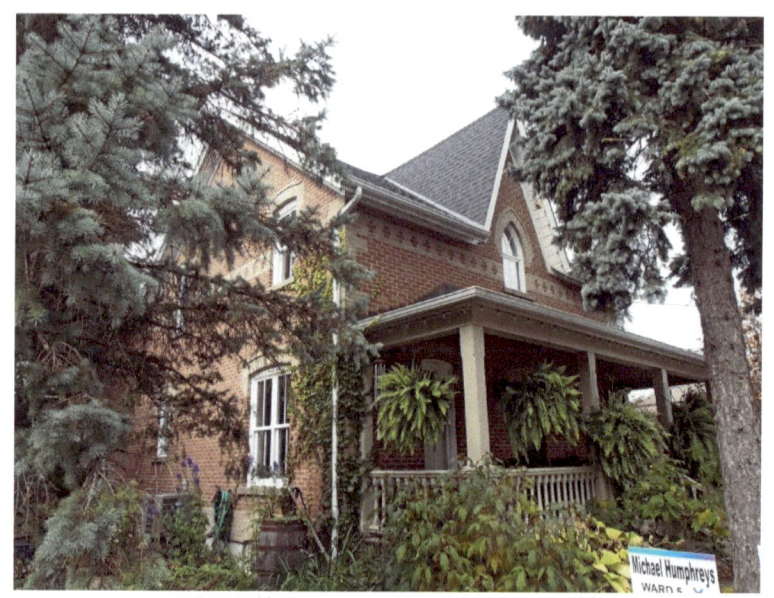

68 Mill Street – Gothic Revival

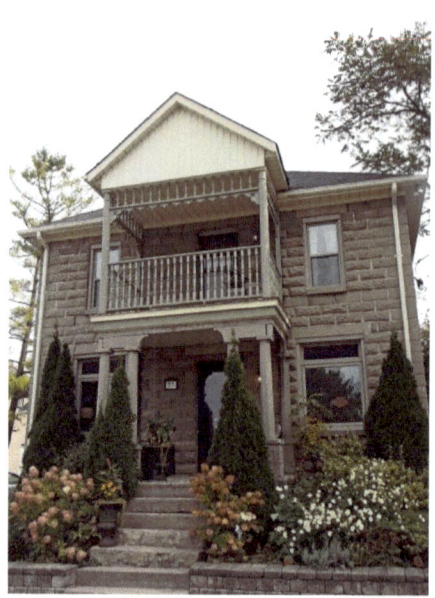

77 Mill Street

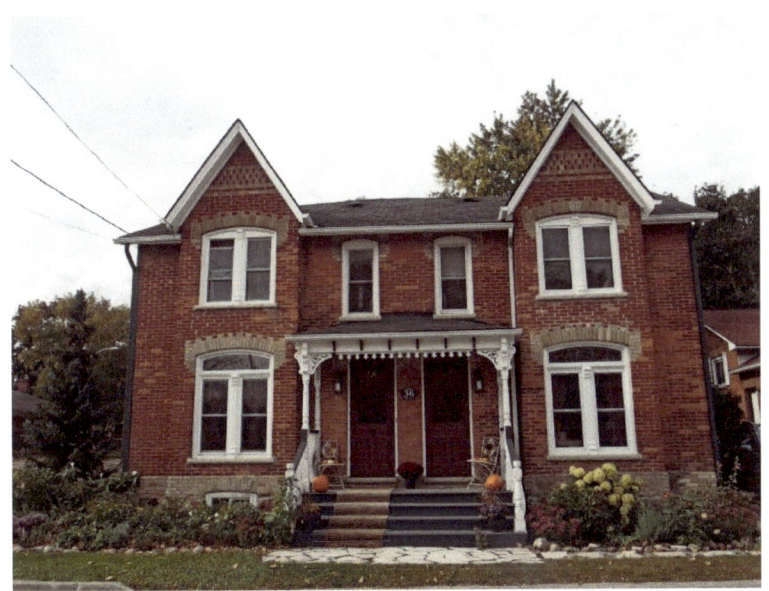

36 Mill Street

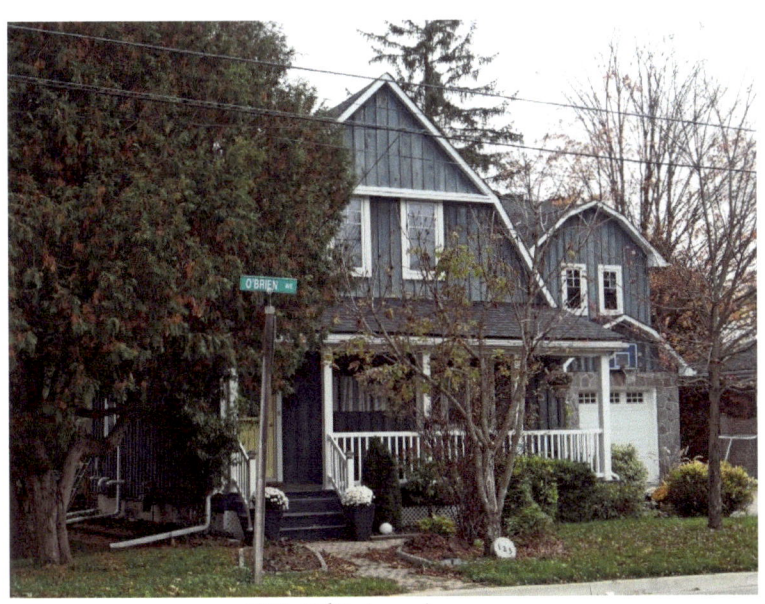

123 O'Brien Avenue

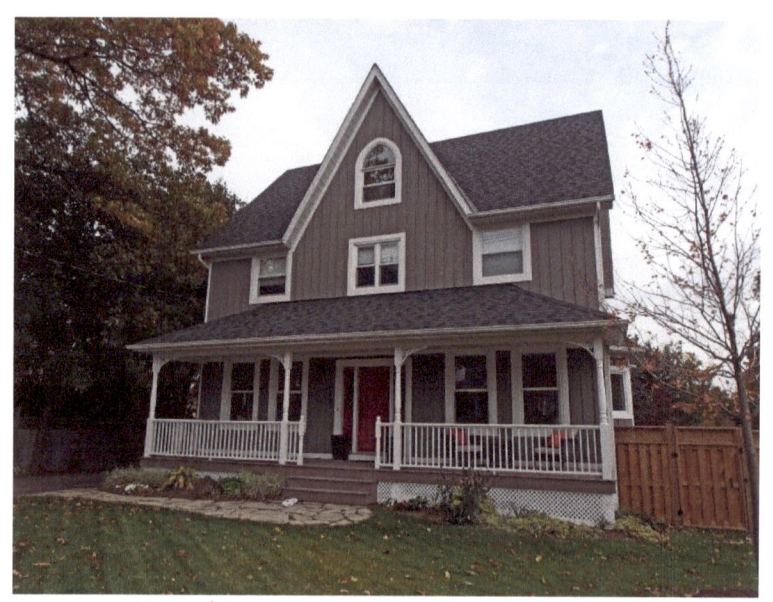
115 O'Brien Avenue – Gothic Revival

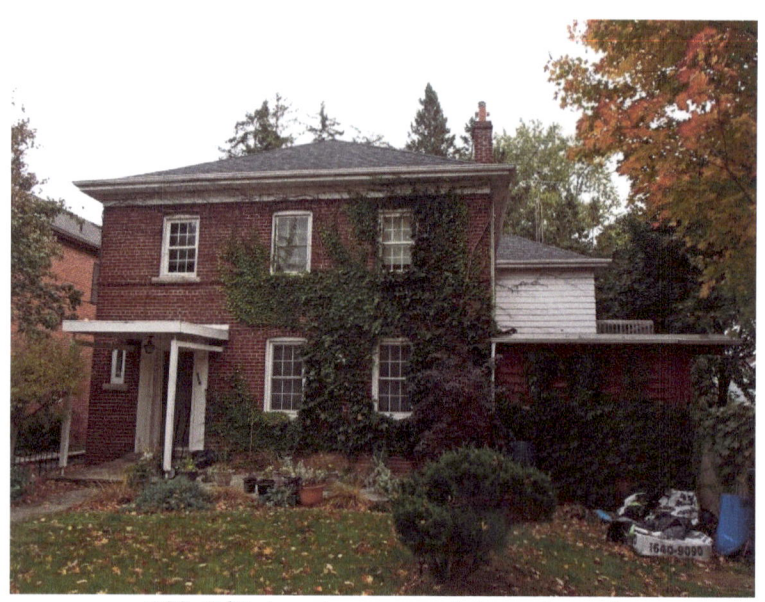
103 O'Brien Avenue – hipped roof

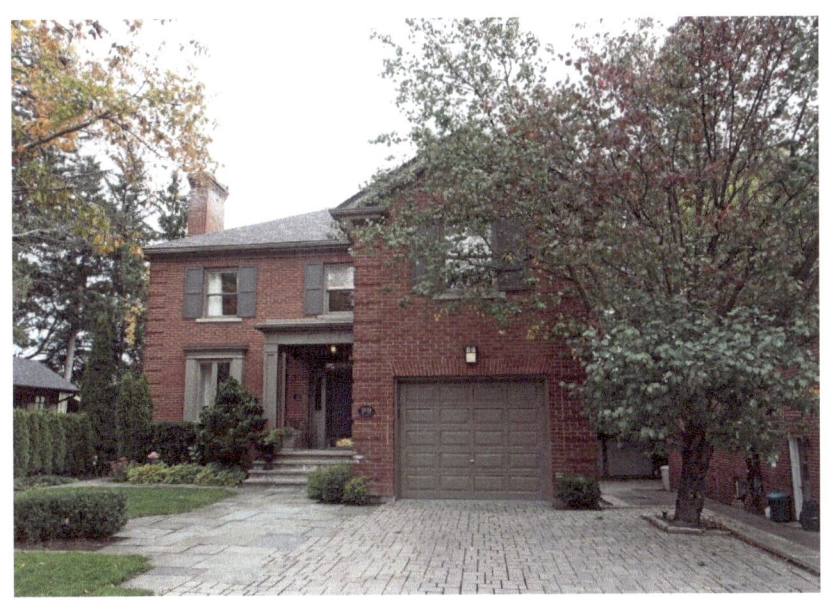

99 O'Brien Avenue

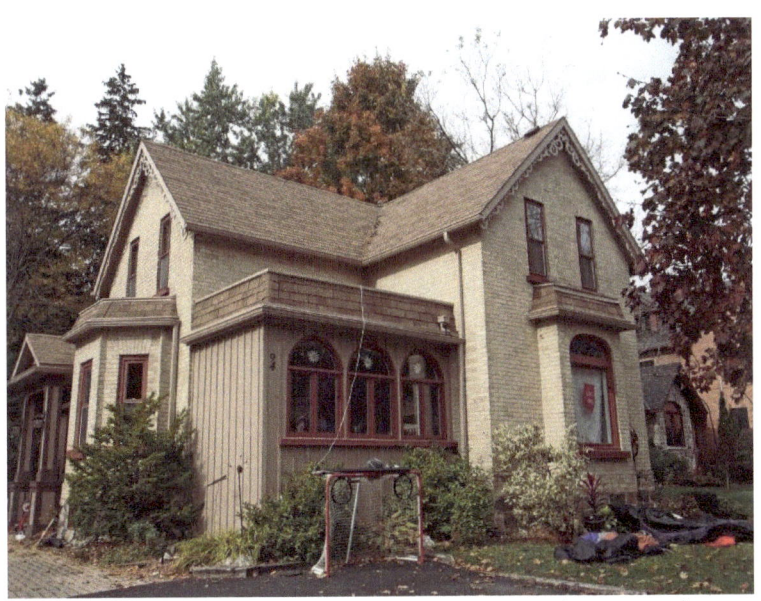

94 O'Brien Avenue – verge board trim, bay windows

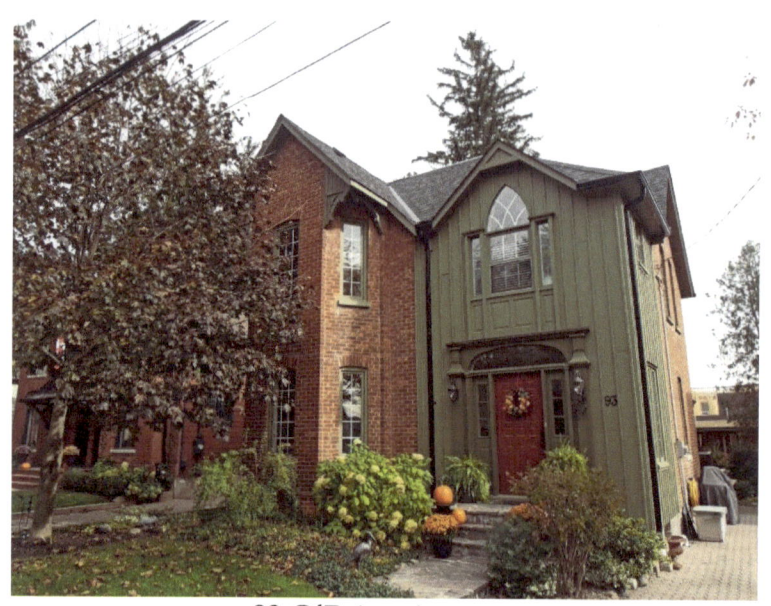

93 O'Brien Avenue

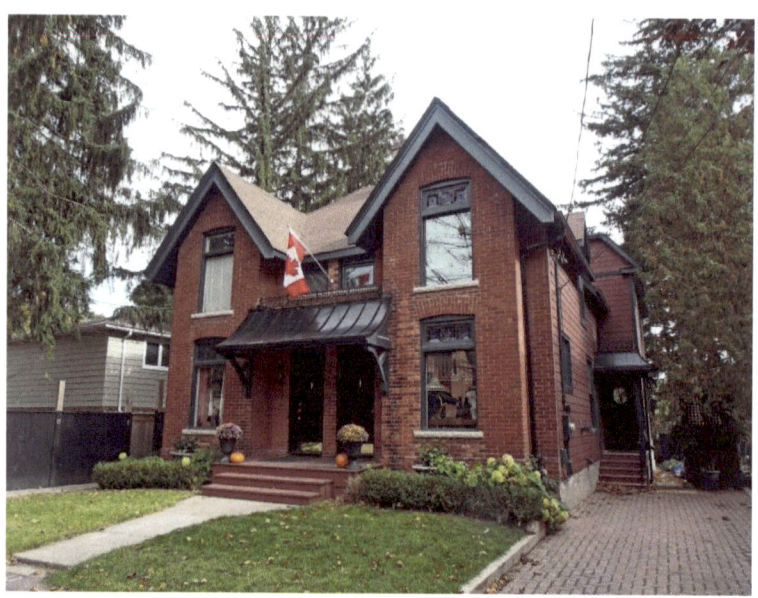

87 O'Brien Avenue

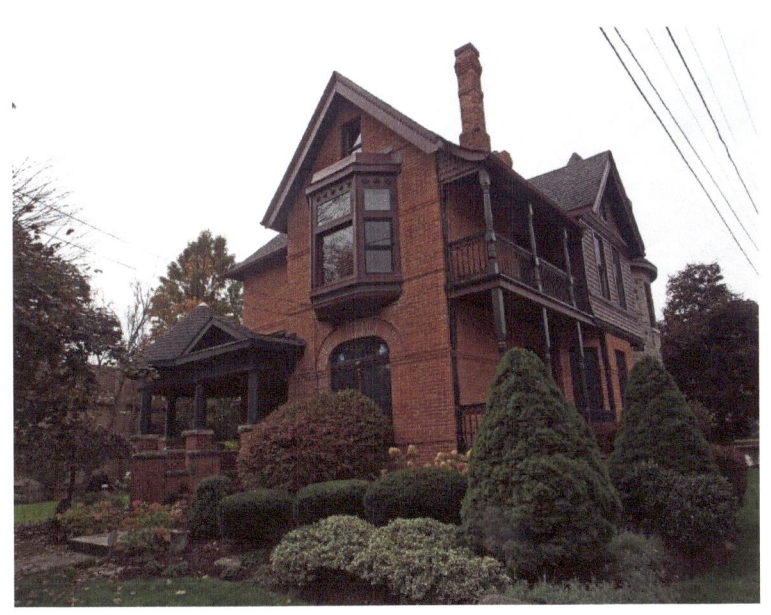

82 O'Brien Avenue – oriel window

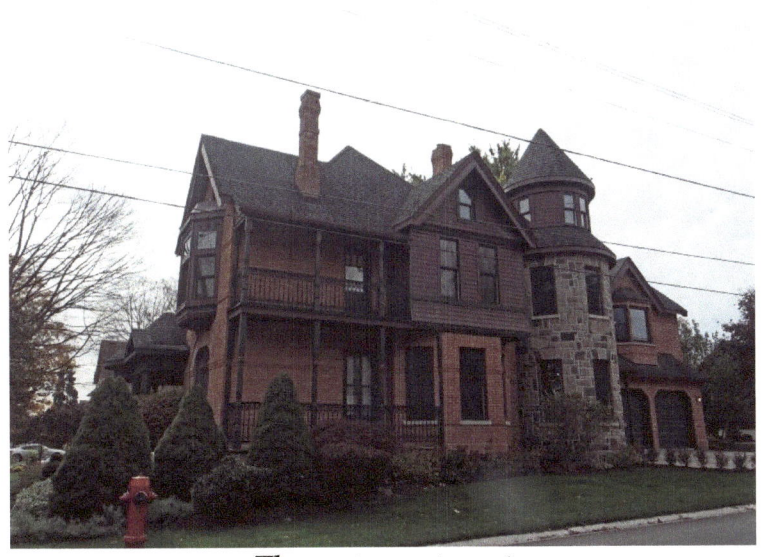

Three storey turret

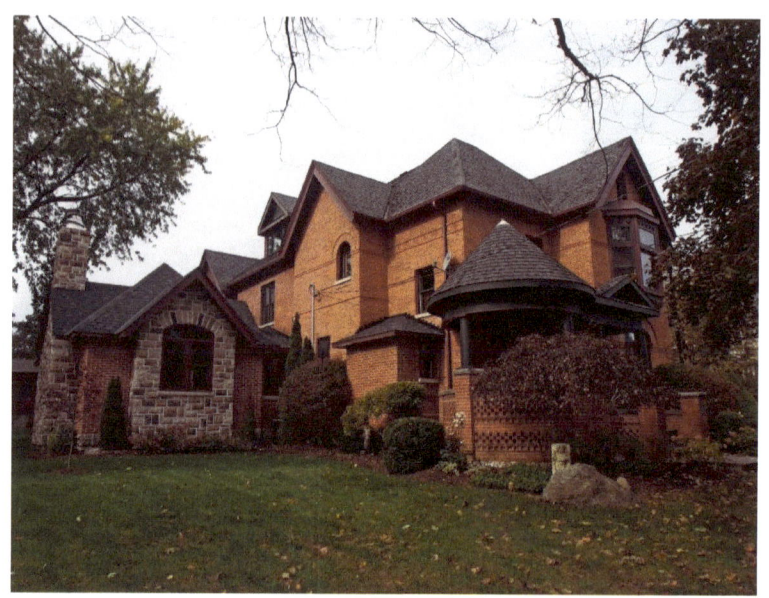

82 O'Brien Avenue

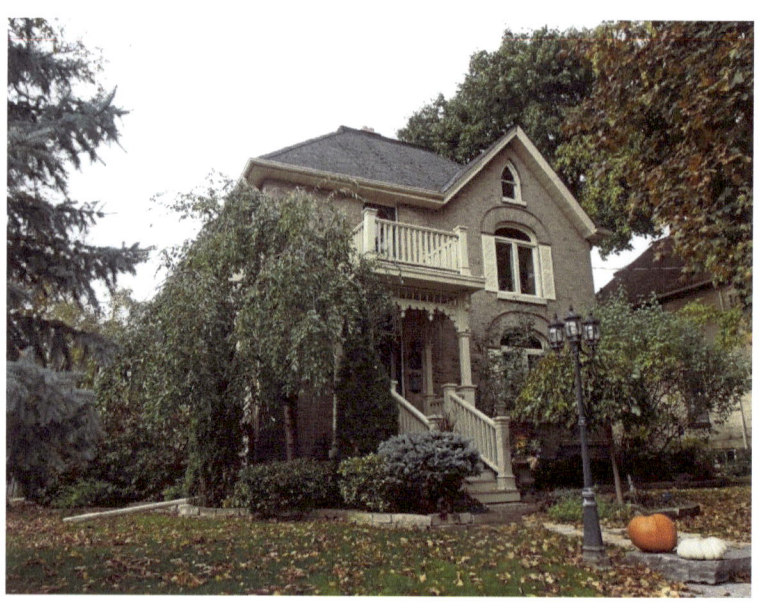

72 O'Brien Avenue

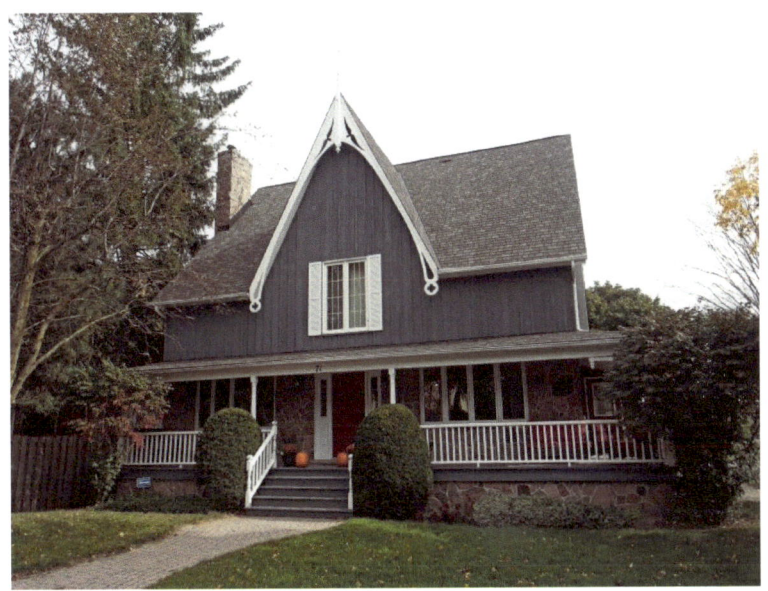

71 O'Brien Avenue

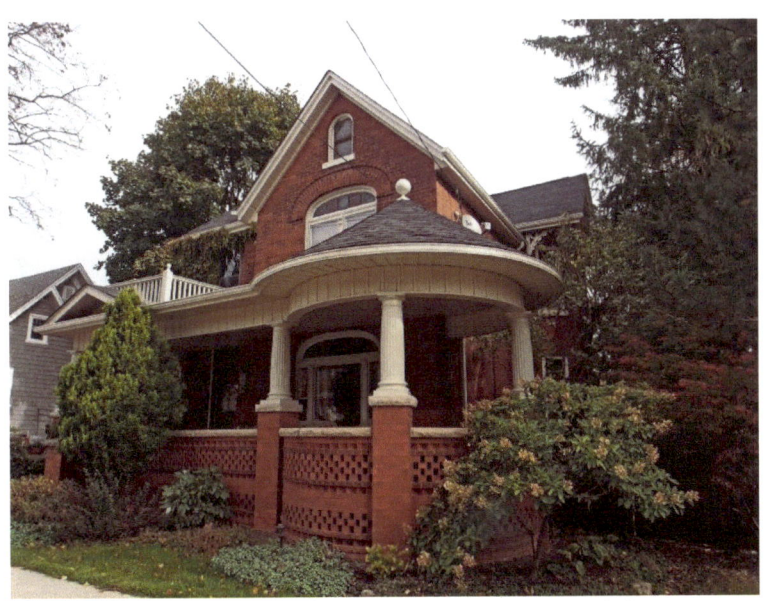

O'Brien Avenue – rounded verandah

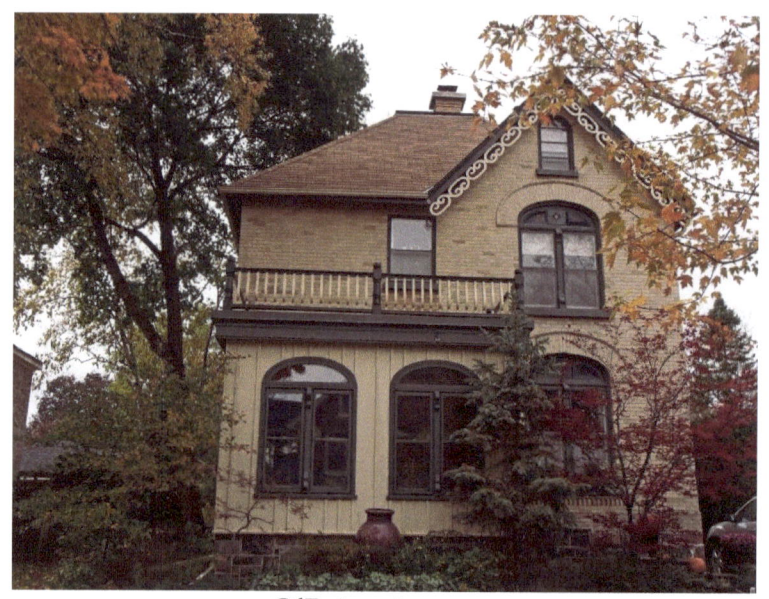

O'Brien Avenue

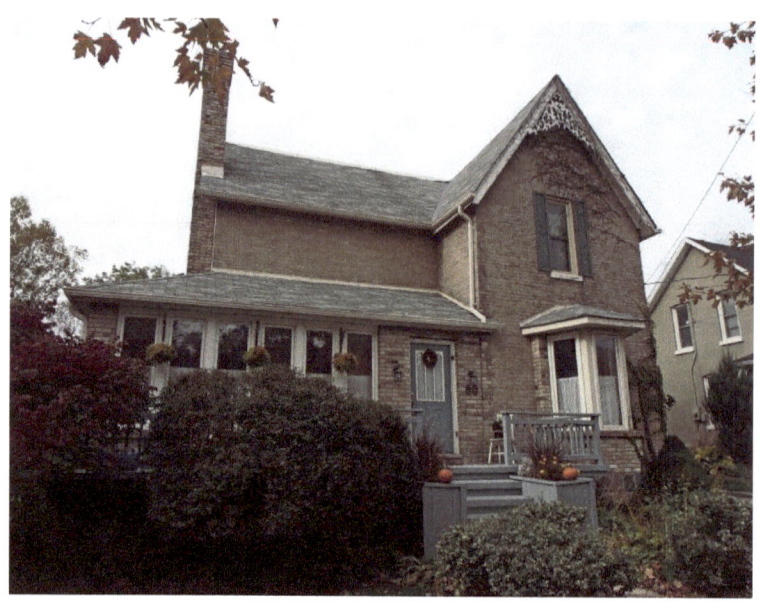

60 O'Brien Avenue

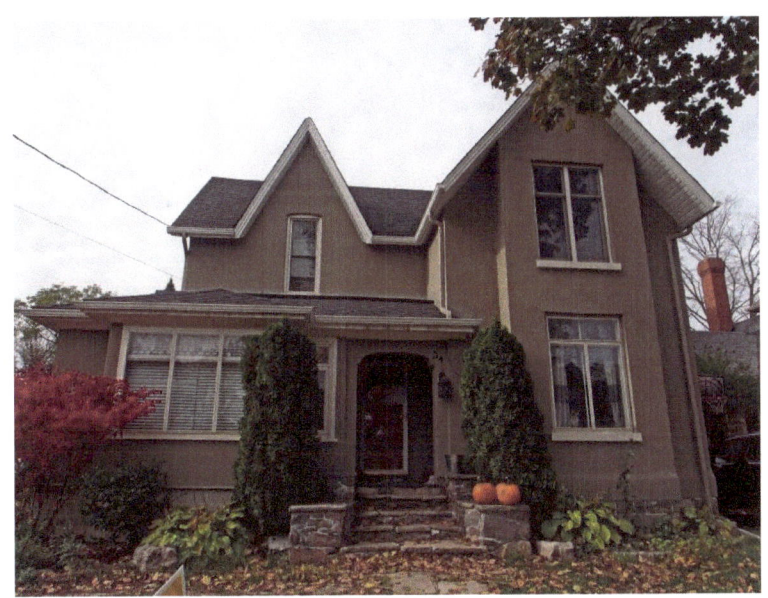

54 O'Brien Avenue

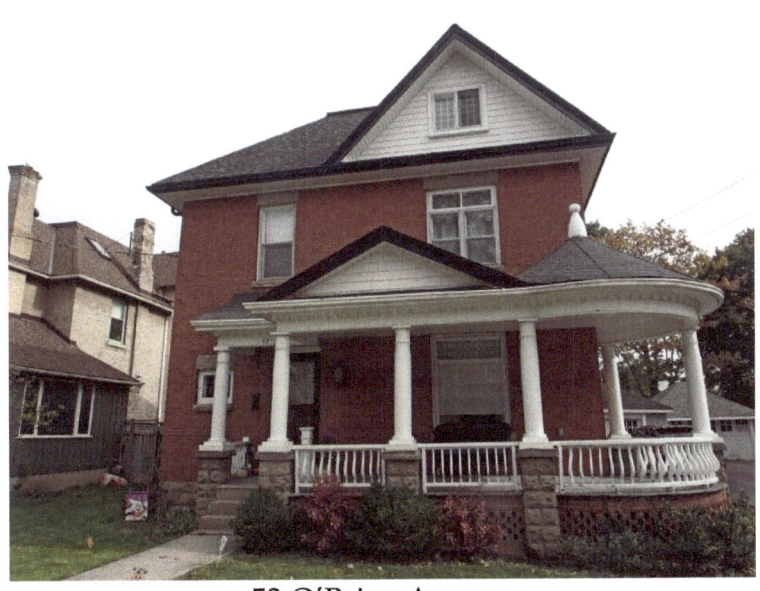

53 O'Brien Avenue

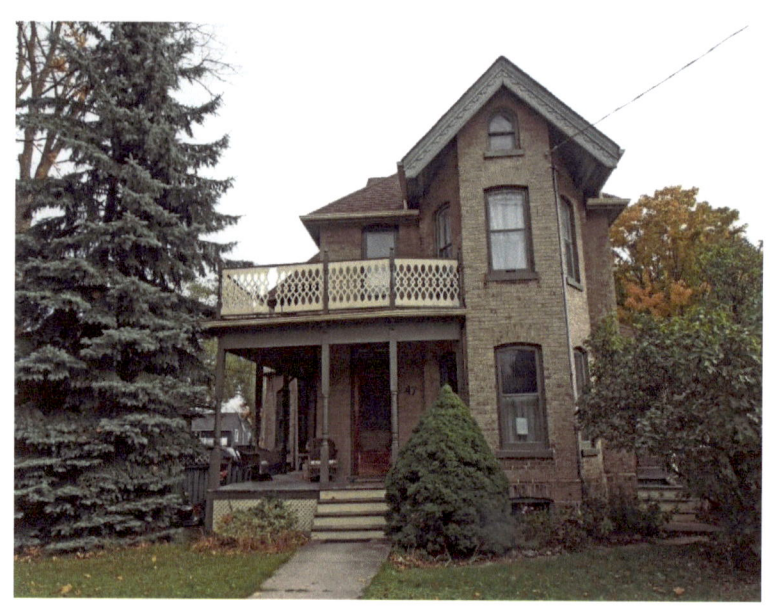

47 O'Brien Avenue

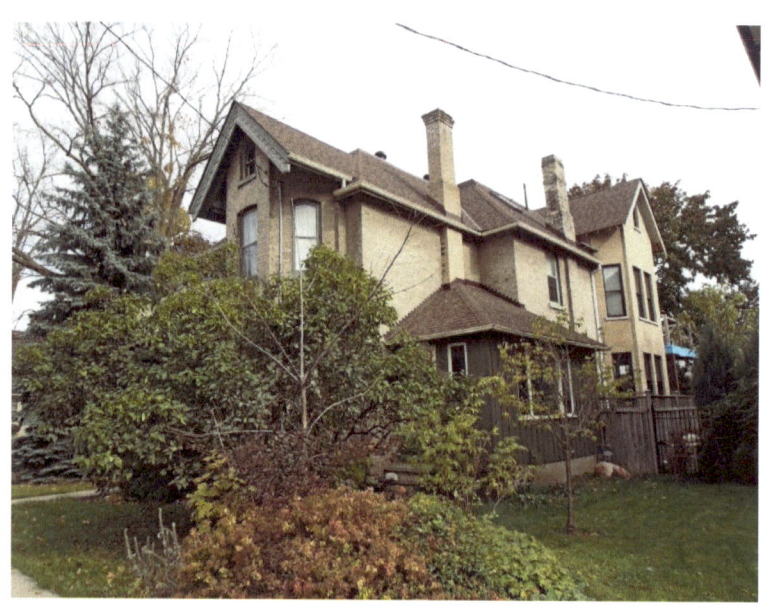

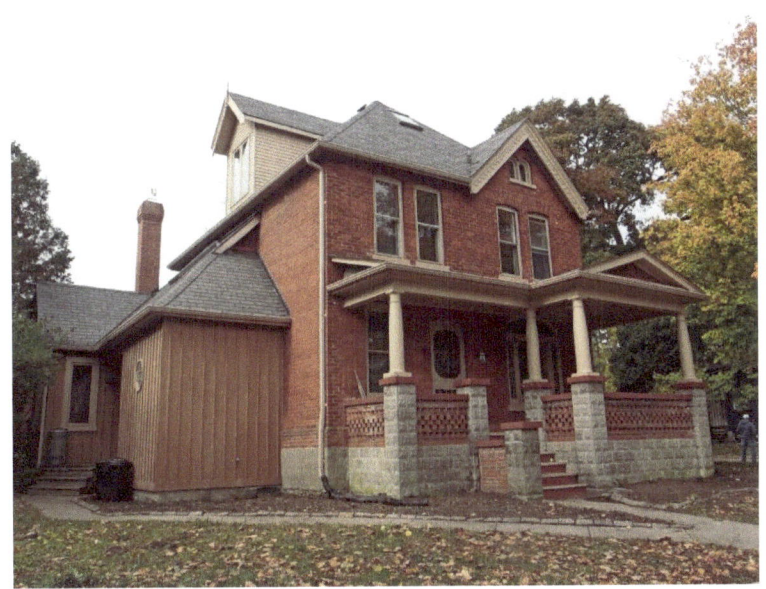

48 O'Brien Avenue

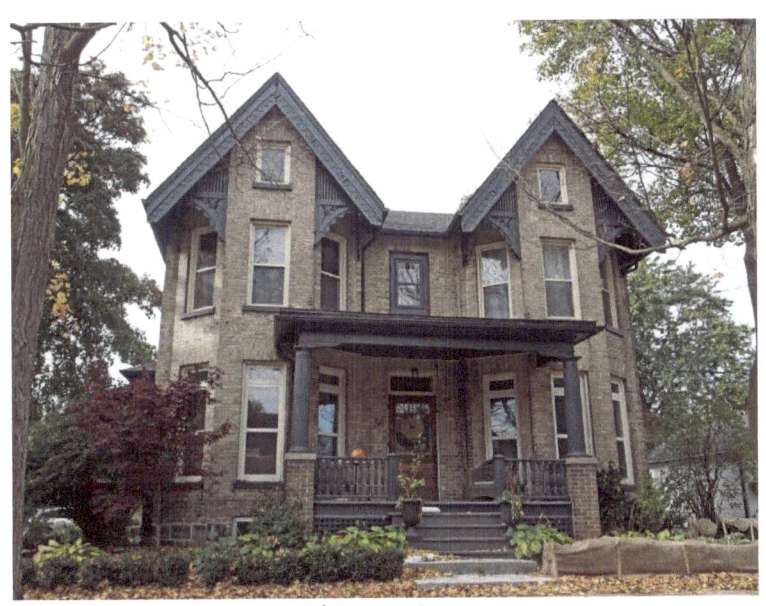

36 O'Brien Avenue

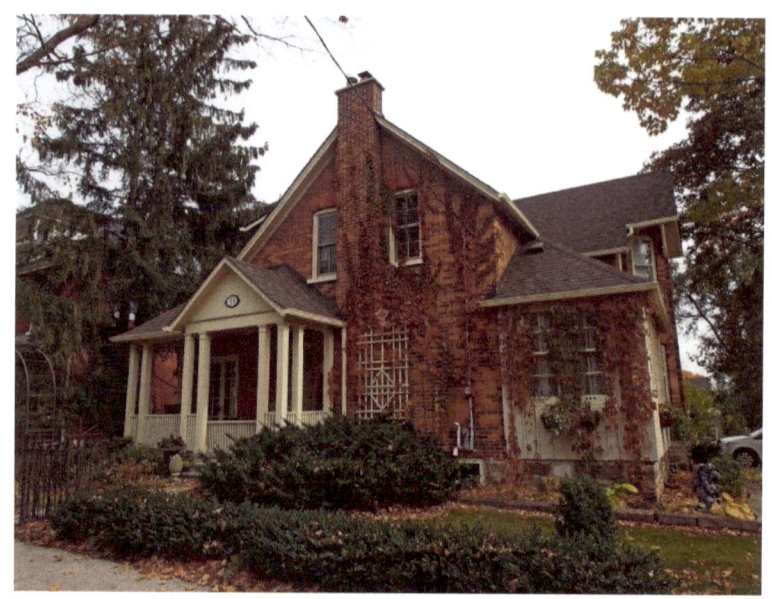

35 O'Brien Avenue

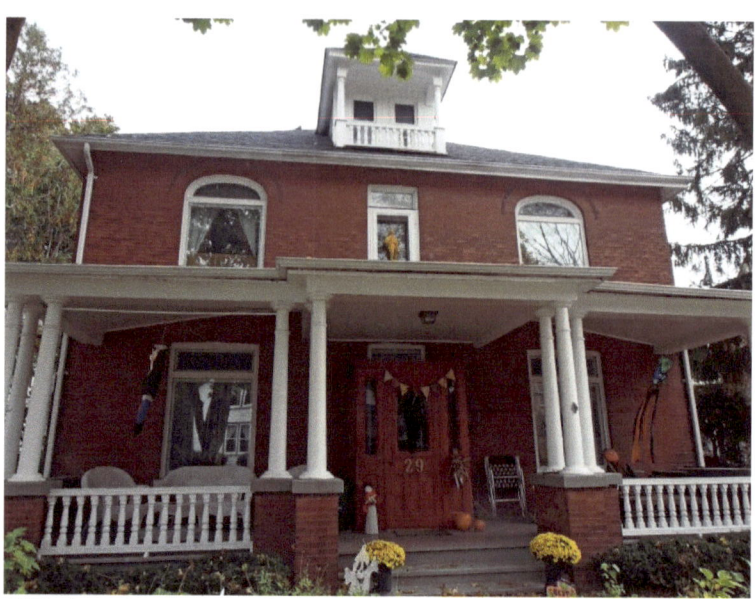

29 O'Brien Avenue – dormer in attic with balcony, transoms above windows

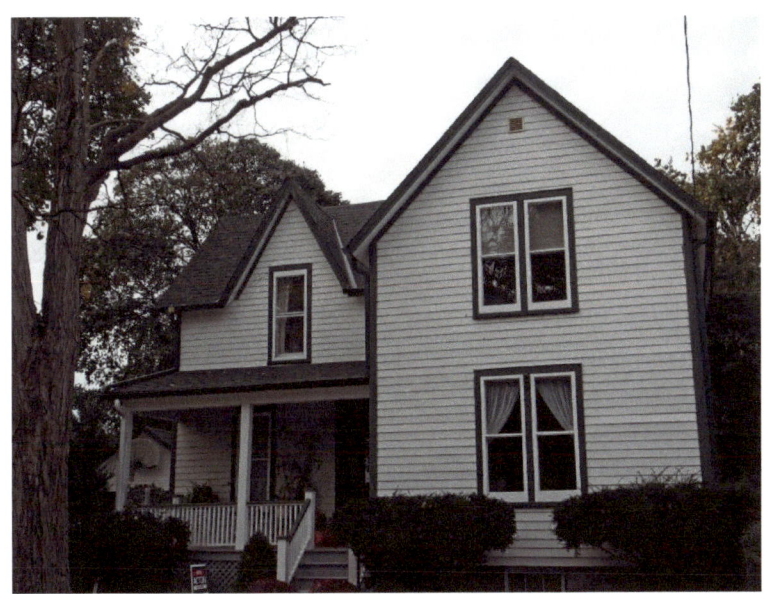

28 O'Brien Avenue

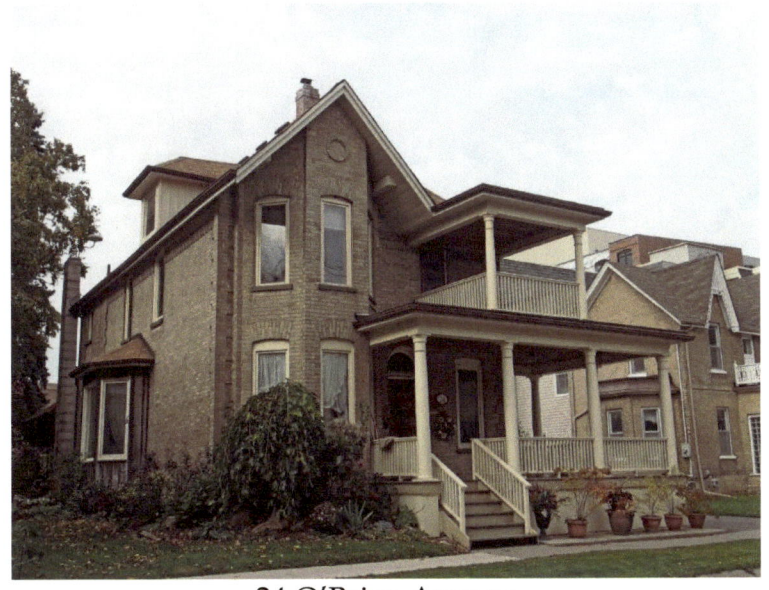

24 O'Brien Avenue

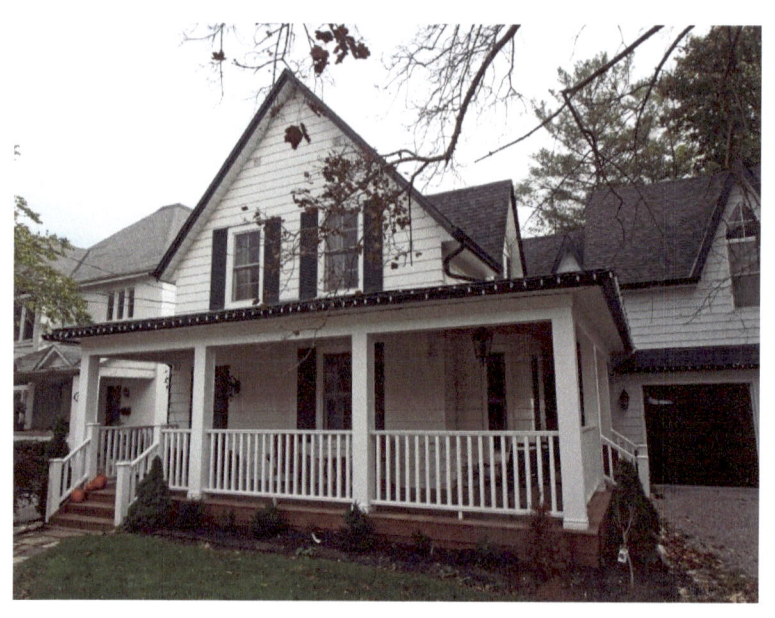

23 O'Brien Avenue

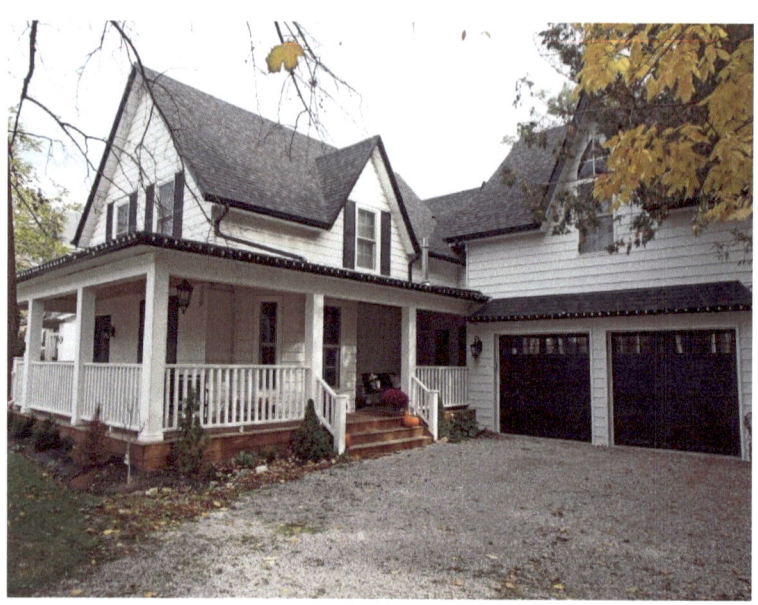

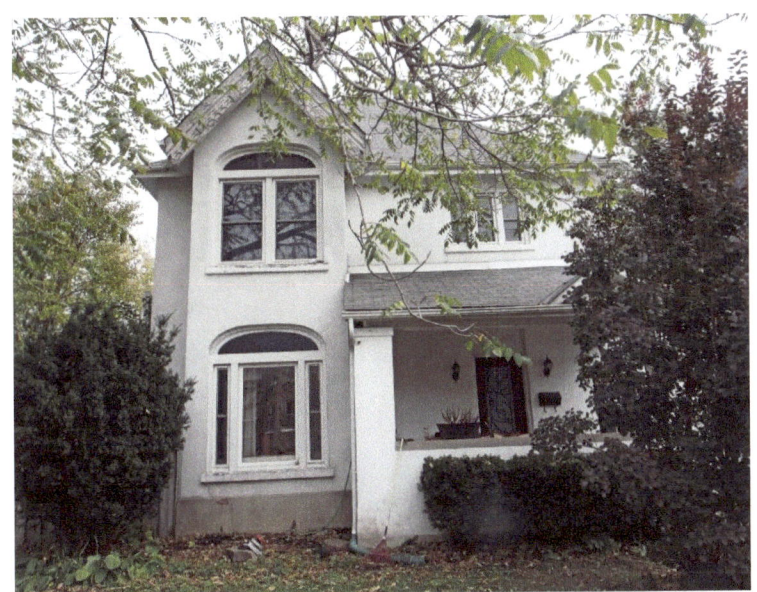

19 O'Brien Avenue

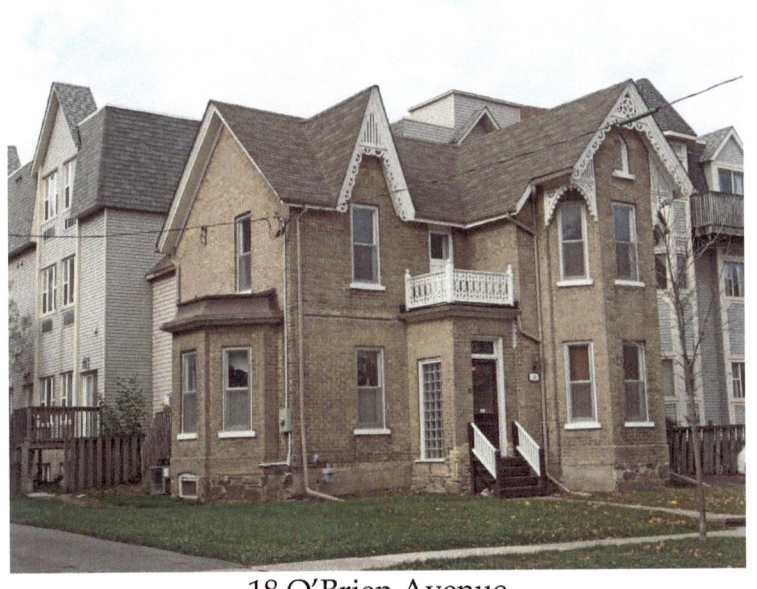

18 O'Brien Avenue

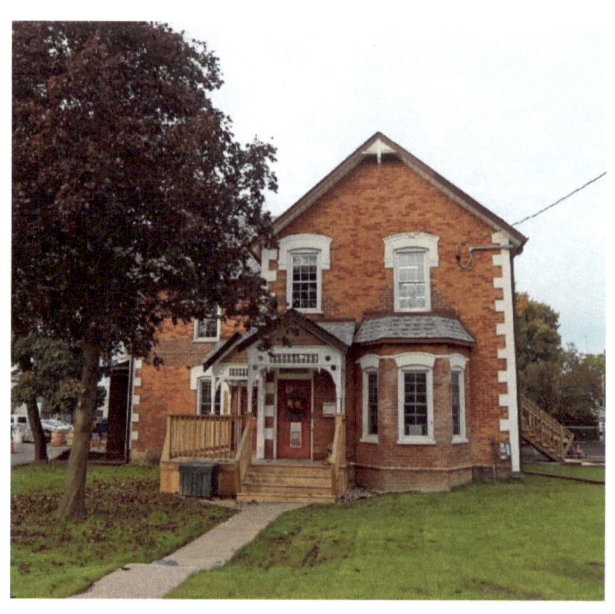

22 Church Street – c. 1880-1885 – Late Victorian Hybrid – built for Lucinda and R.J. Daley, a shoe merchant – corner quoins, bay window

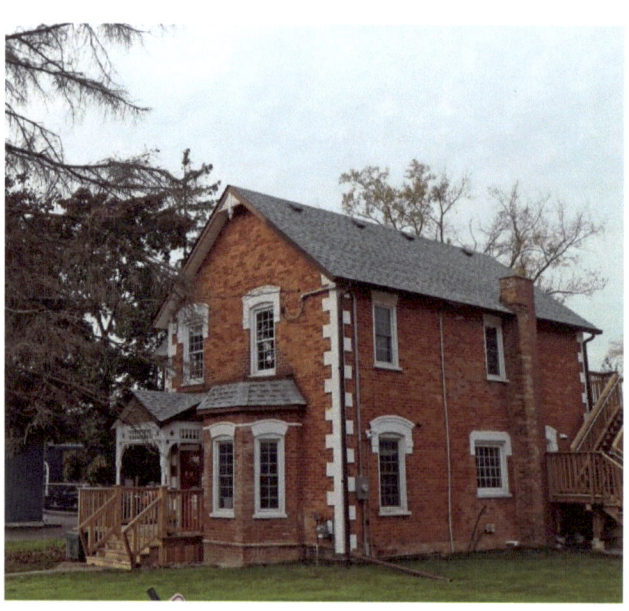

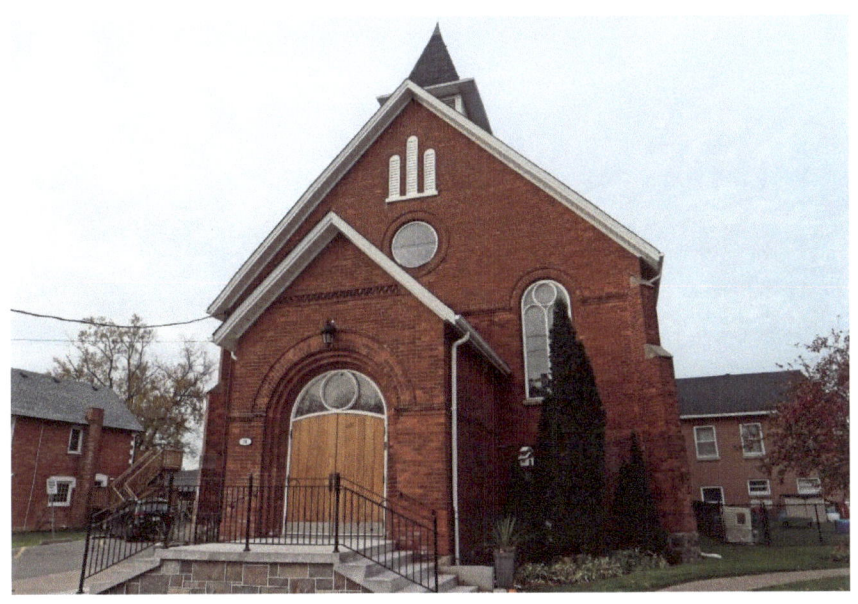

34 Church Street – Stouffville United Church (originally Methodist) – 1892 – Romanesque/Gothic Revival

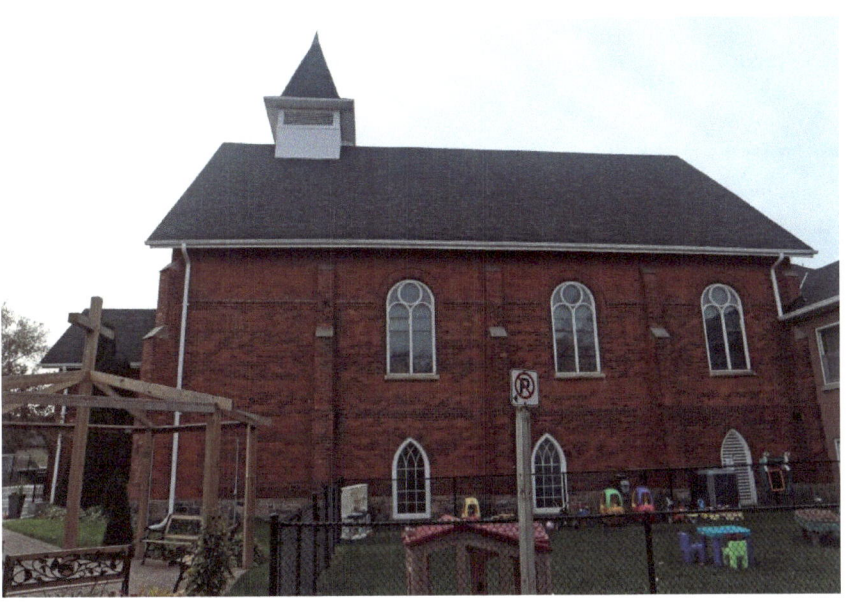

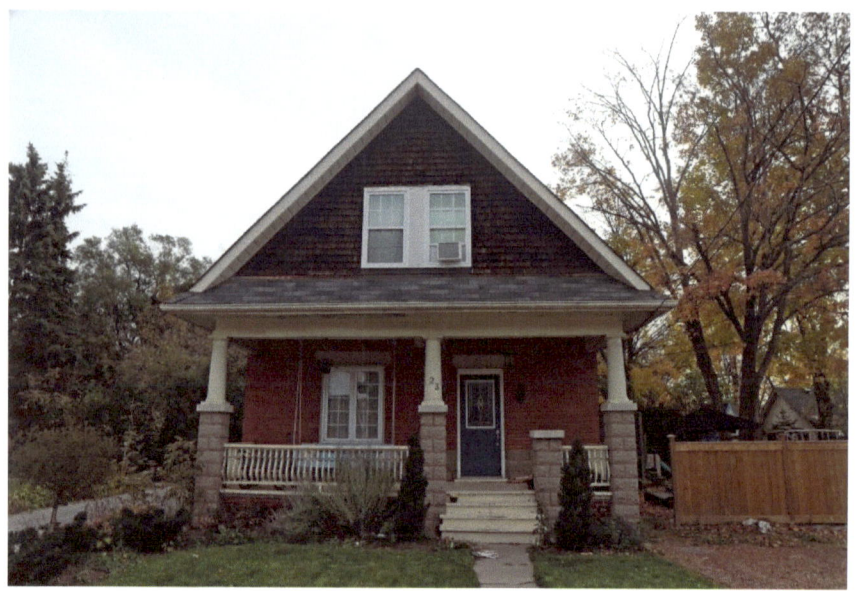

23 Church Street

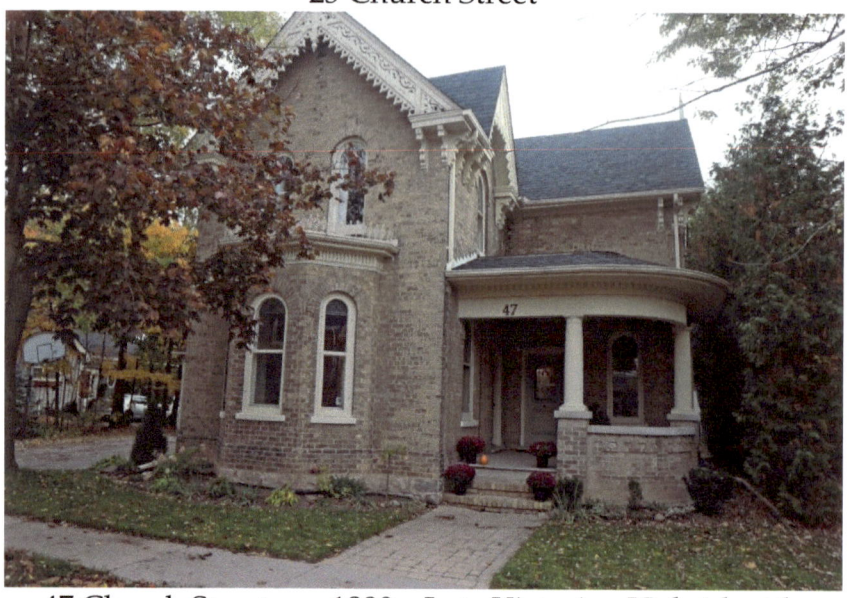

47 Church Street – c. 1890 – Late Victorian Hybrid with Italianate features, verge board trim and finial on gables, bay window, rounded verandah added in late 1920s – built by farmer William Mason for himself and wife Margaret Rae

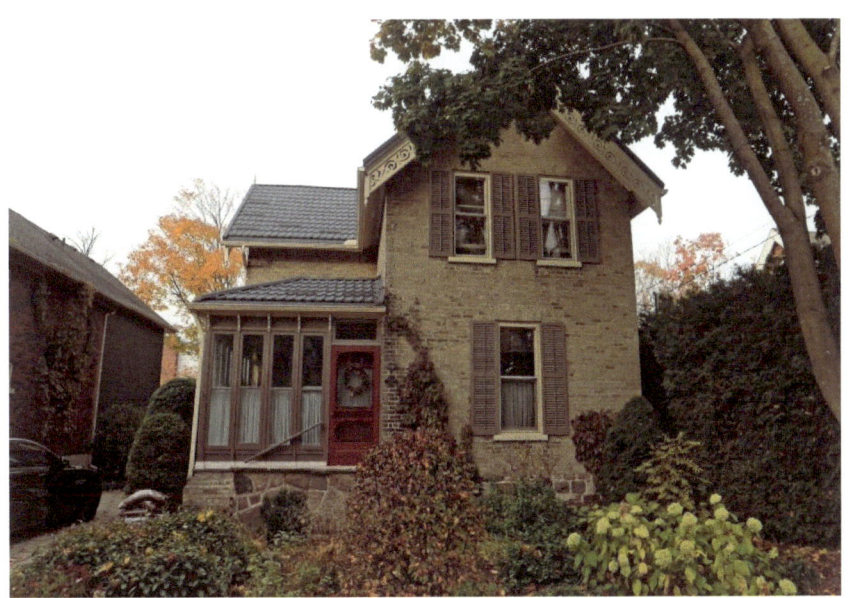

50 Church Street – 1889 – Late Victorian Hybrid with original enclosed porch – owned by Mr. and Mrs. William Sylvester (hardware merchant), then home of Lemon sisters, Jessie and Mary

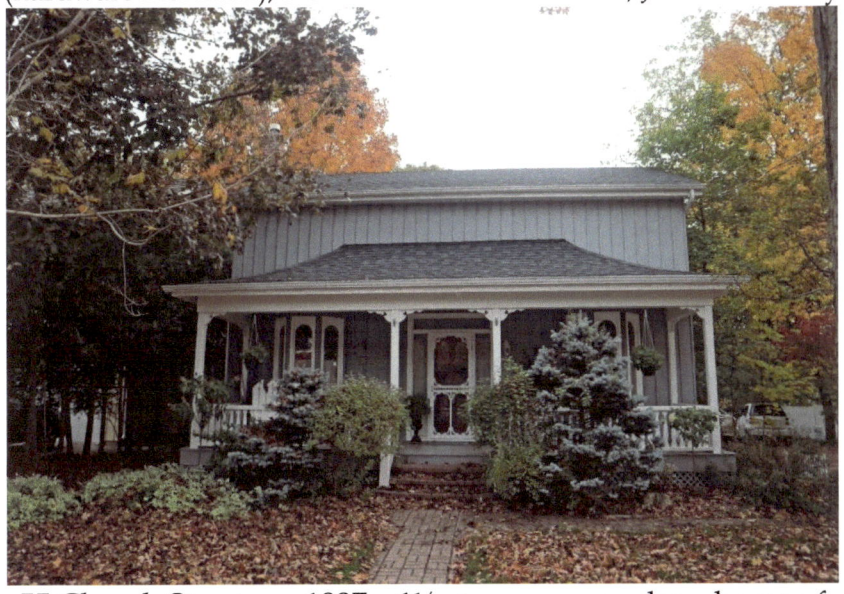

55 Church Street – c. 1887 – 1½ storey vernacular – home of Nelson Connor, retired farmer

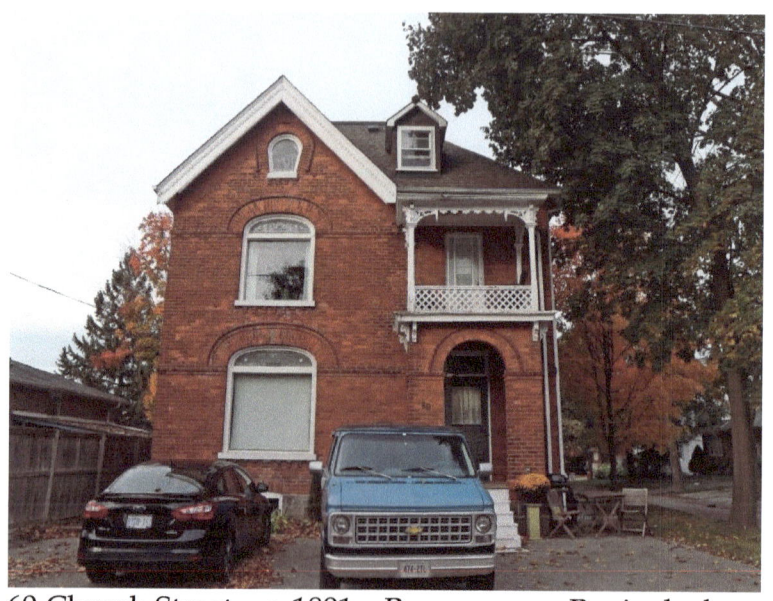

60 Church Street – c. 1891 – Romanesque Revival – long known as the David Stouffer house – he was a village historian and grandson of the founder of Stouffville, Abraham Stouffer – corbelled brick string courses around voussoirs, stained glass window transoms, second floor balcony

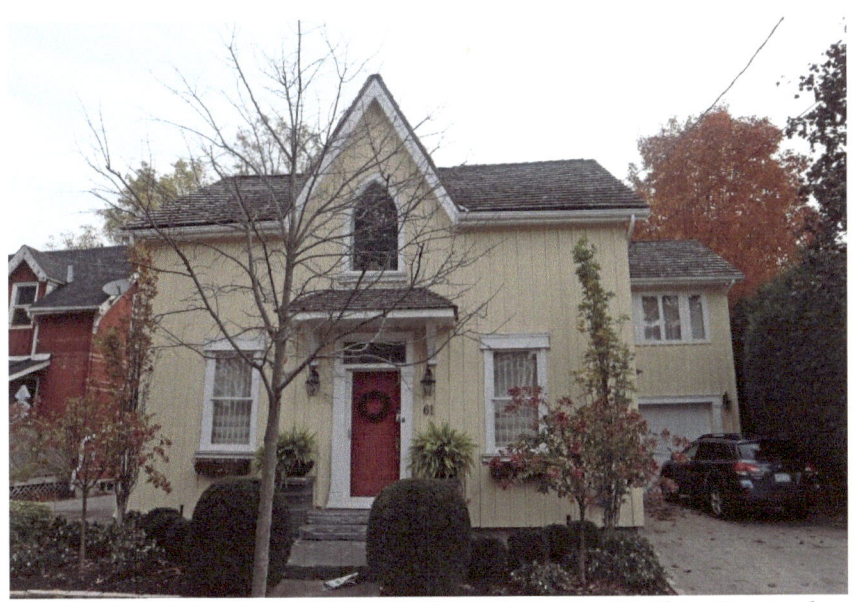

61 Church Street – c. 1878-1882 – 1½ storey Gothic Revival – George and Harriet James bought the house in 1882. The house has board and batten cladding.

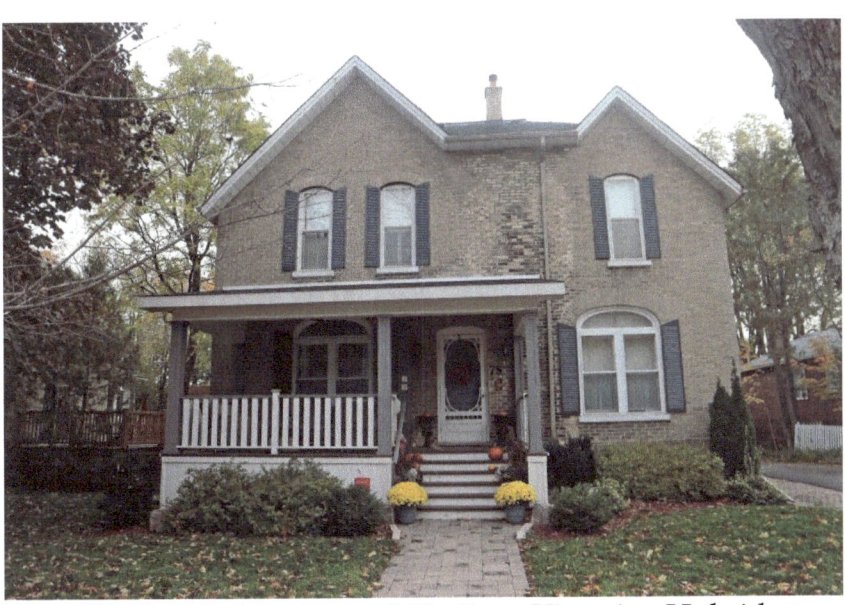

75 Church Street – c. 1895 – Late Victorian Hybrid

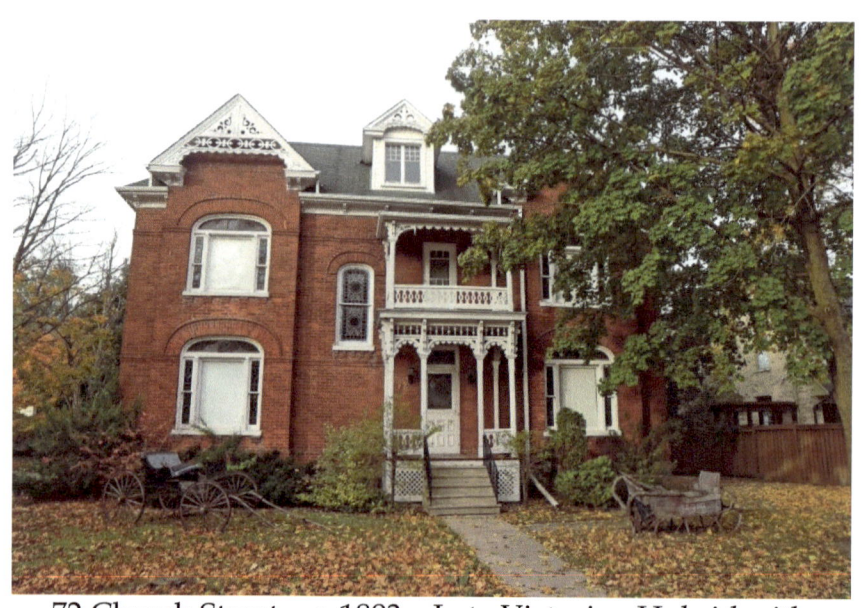

72 Church Street – c. 1893 – Late Victorian Hybrid with Romanesque Revival and Italianate details - corbelled brick string courses around voussoirs, stained glass window transoms and sidelights, double storey porch, dormer, decorative woodwork on brackets, gingerbread and porches

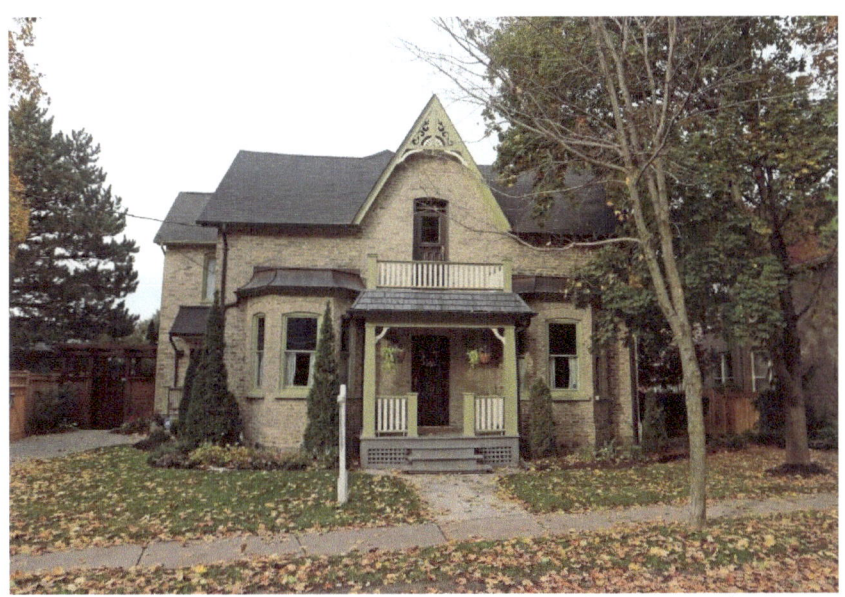

80 Church Street – c. 1889 – 1½ storey Gothic Revival – built for Isaac Broadway (a drugstore owner) and his wife

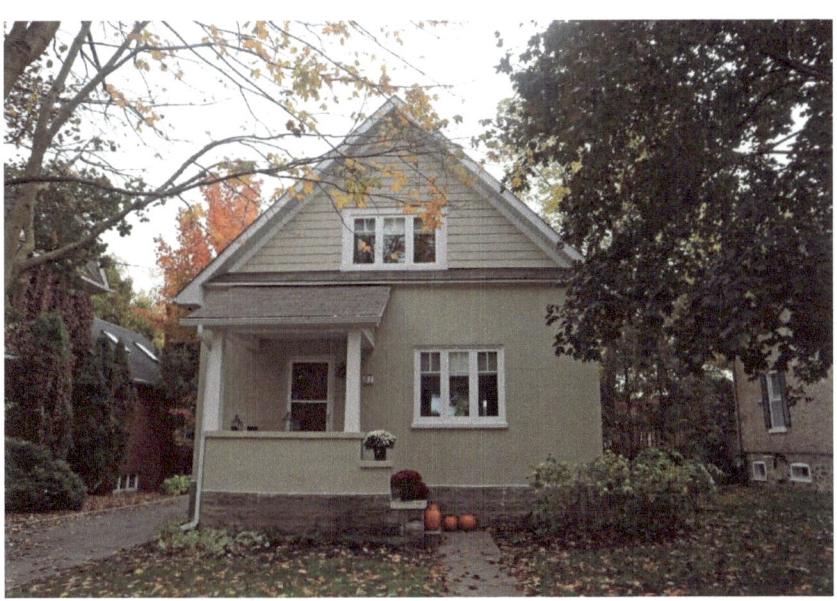

81 Church Street

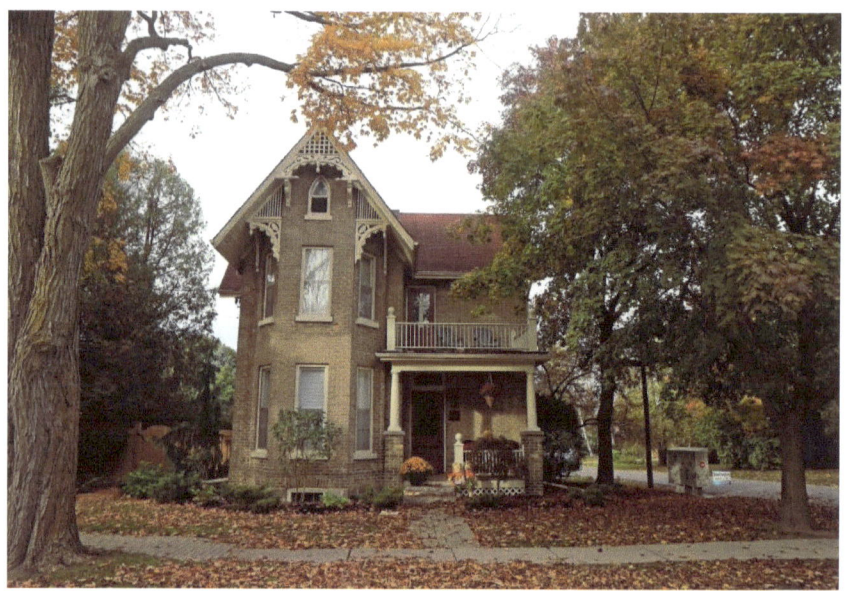

86 Church Street – c. 1885 – Late Victorian Hybrid with bay and gable – home of Samuel and Mary Warriner, boot and shoe store merchant – open porch with balcony above, fretwork, gingerbread

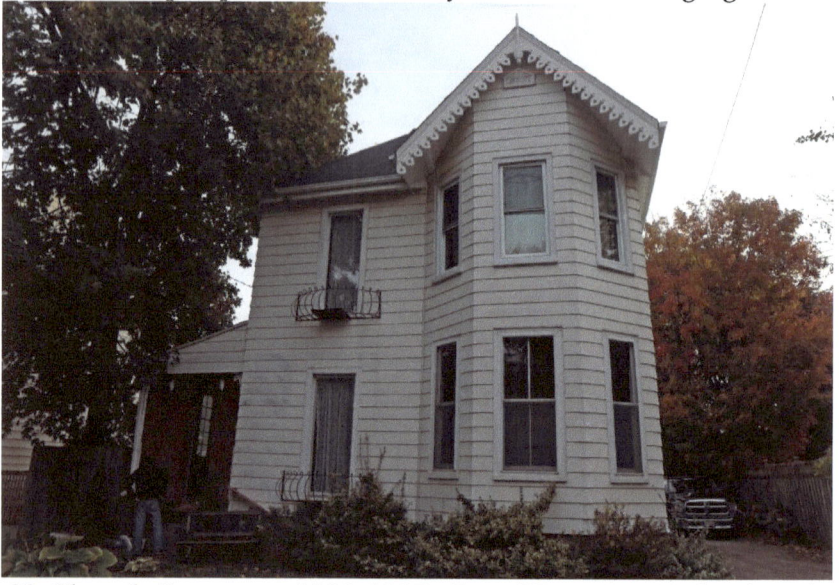

93 Church Street – c. 1890-1895 - Late Victorian Hybrid with bay and gable, finial and decorated fascia

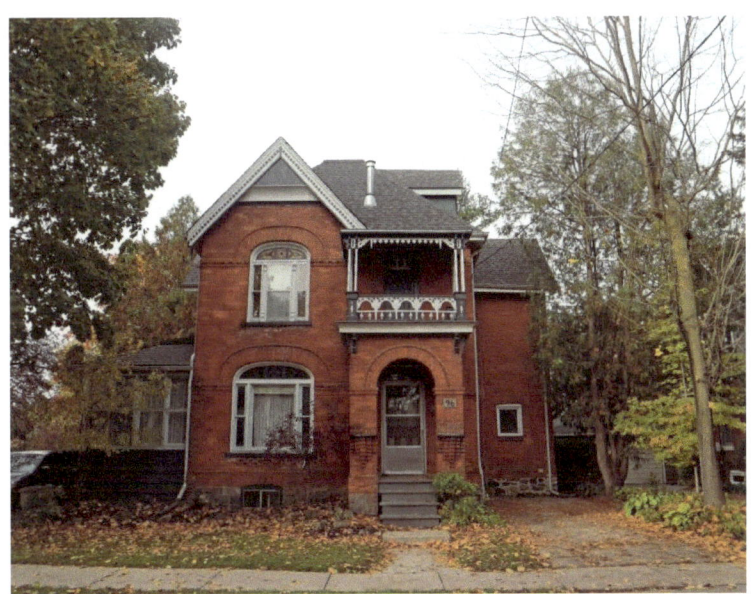

96 Church Street – c. 1890 – Romanesque/Queen Anne – built by Nathan Forsyth as his residence, local master builder - corbelled brick string course, balcony over verandah

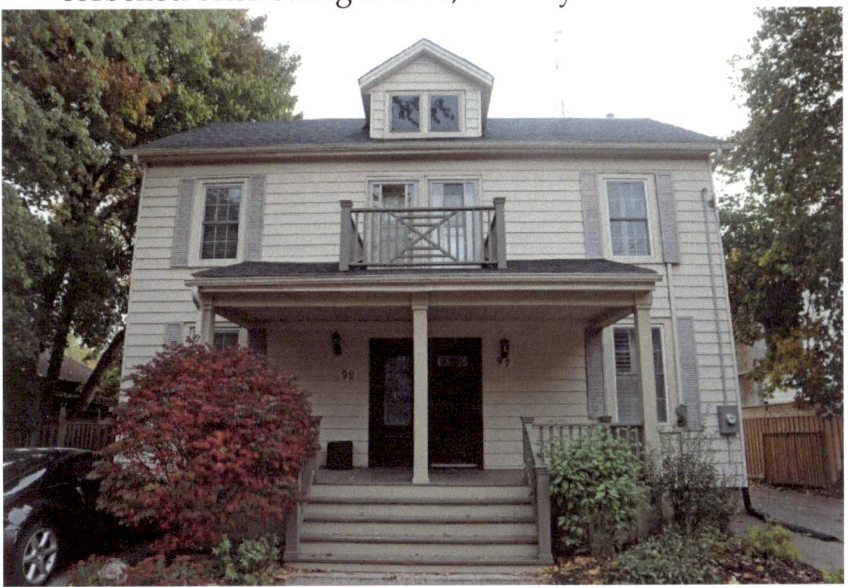

97-99 Church Street – c. 1870 – Georgian – balcony over open verandah

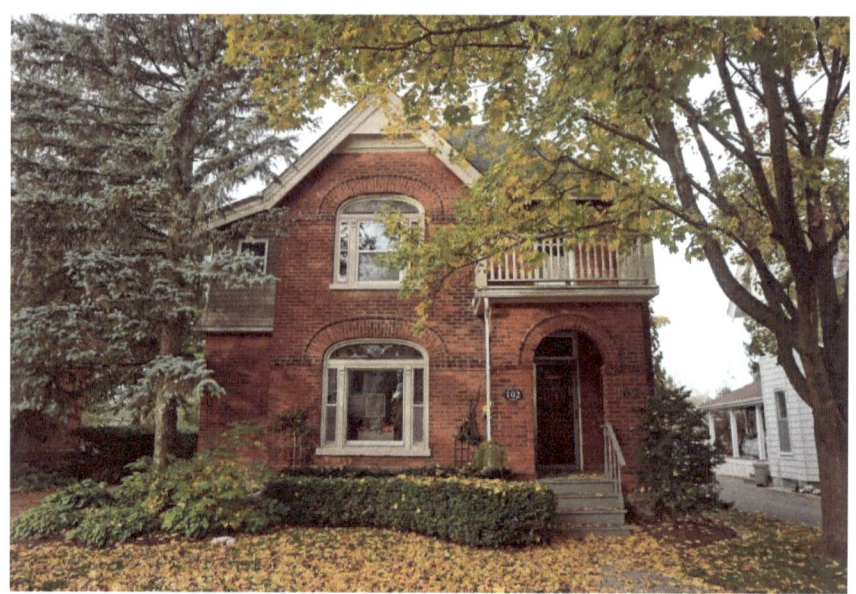

102 Church Street – c. 1893-1904 – Romanesque Revival – built by Nathan Forsyth – brick porch with balcony above

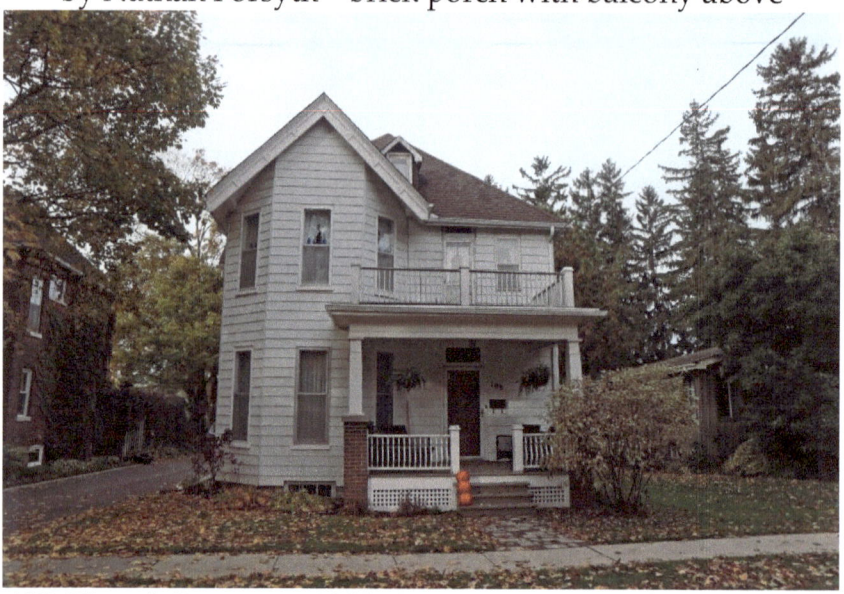

108 Church Street – c. 1890 - Late Victorian Hybrid with bay and gable – built for Hiram Johnson, bakeshop owner – open verandah with open balcony above

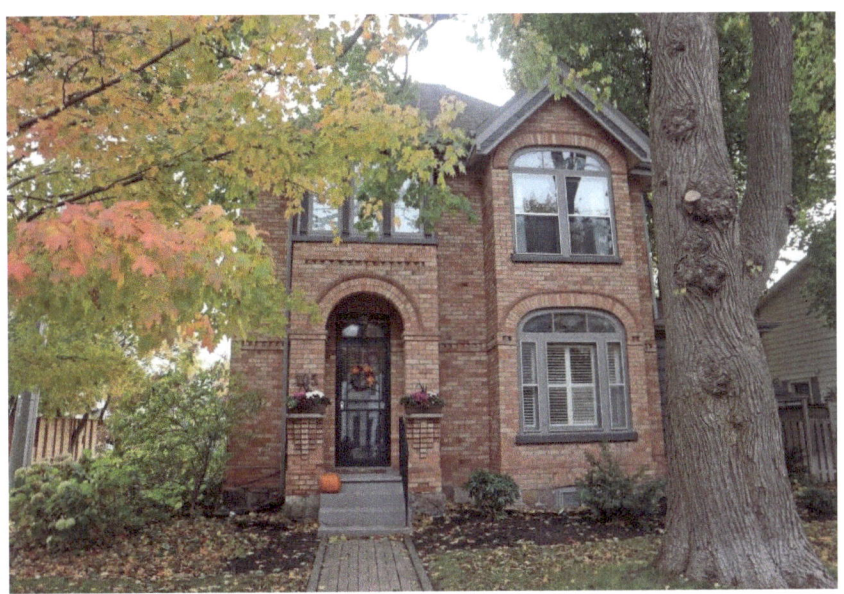

105 Church Street – c. 1893 – Romanesque Revival – built by Nathan Forsyth for John Monkhouse, tailor – decorative brick detail on the diagonal string course, brick shelves either side of the door for plants

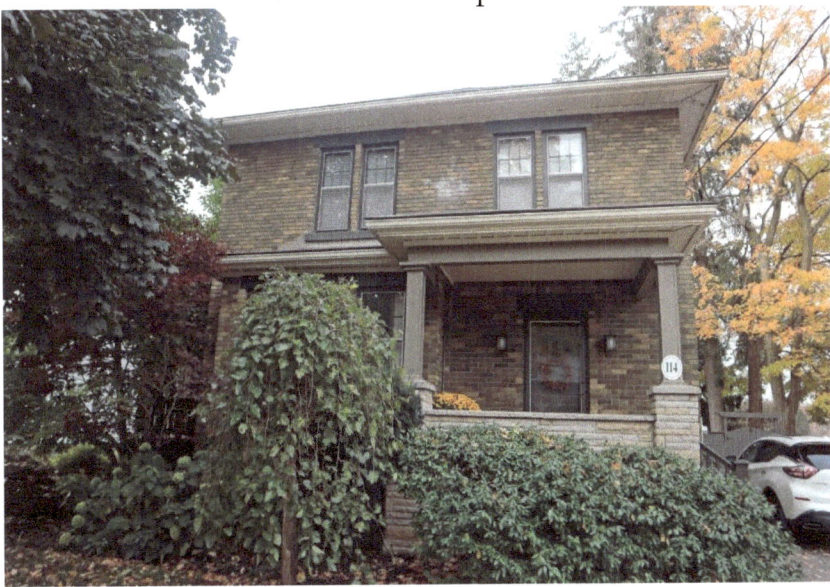

114 Church Street

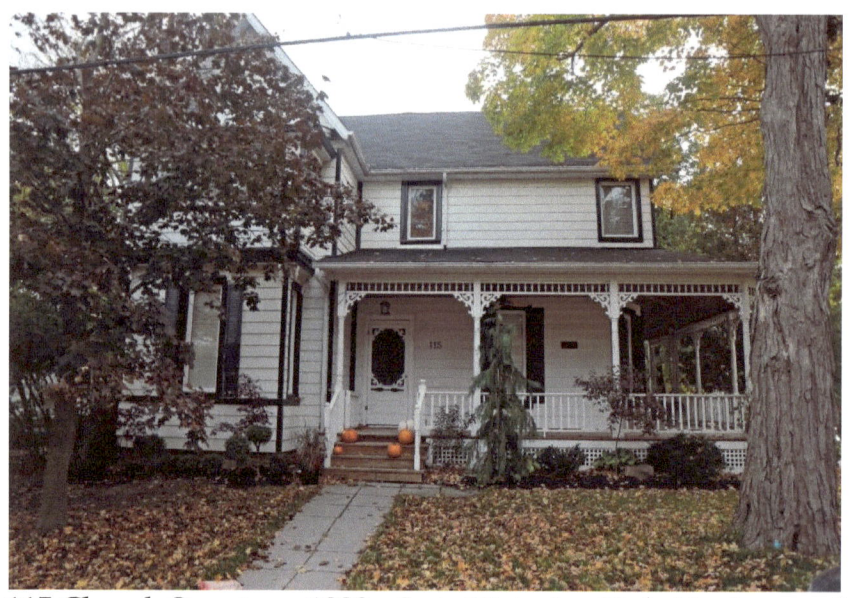

115 Church Street – c. 1889 – Late Victorian Hybrid – home of John and Margaret McDonald, manager of Edward Wheeler's farm – wraparound verandah

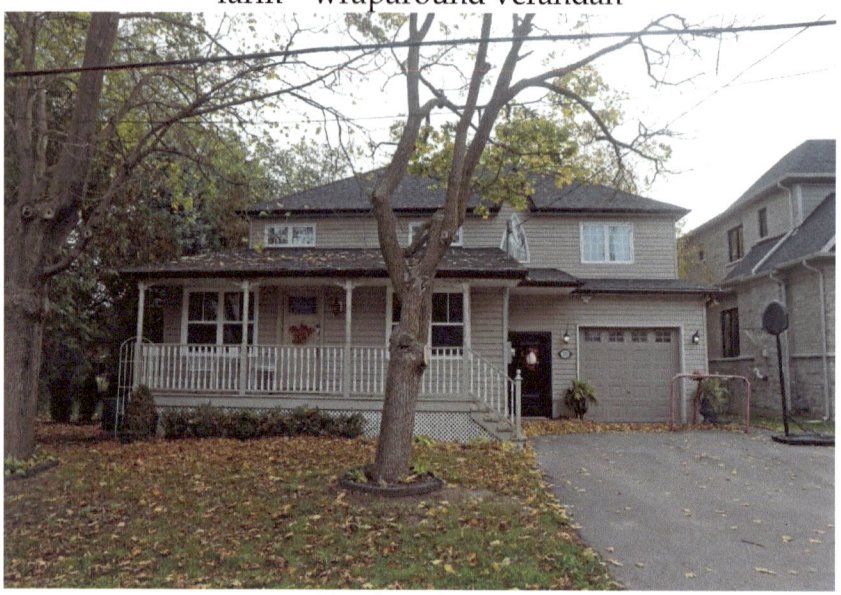

133 Church Street

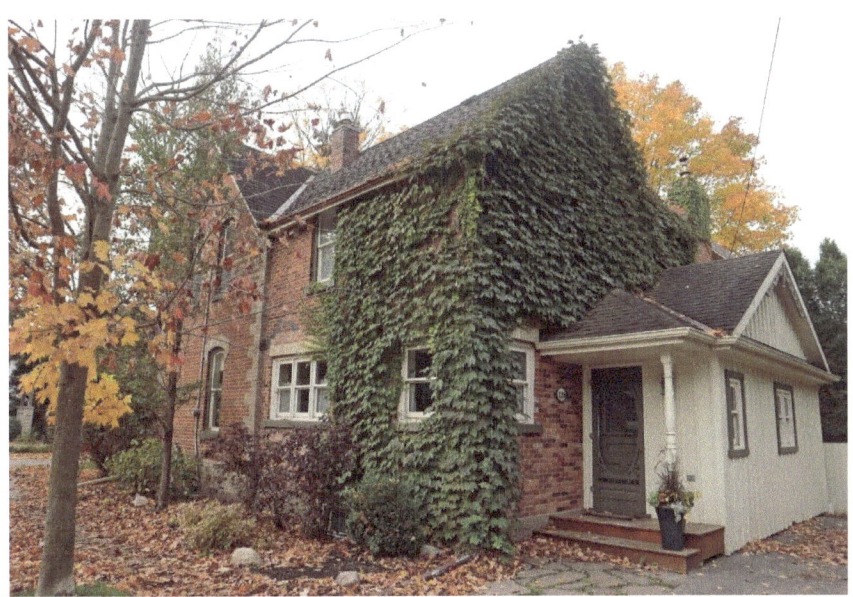

126 Church Street – c. 1870 - Late Victorian Hybrid – assumed to be home of Edward Wheeler, land, mill and business owner – corner quoins, voussoirs

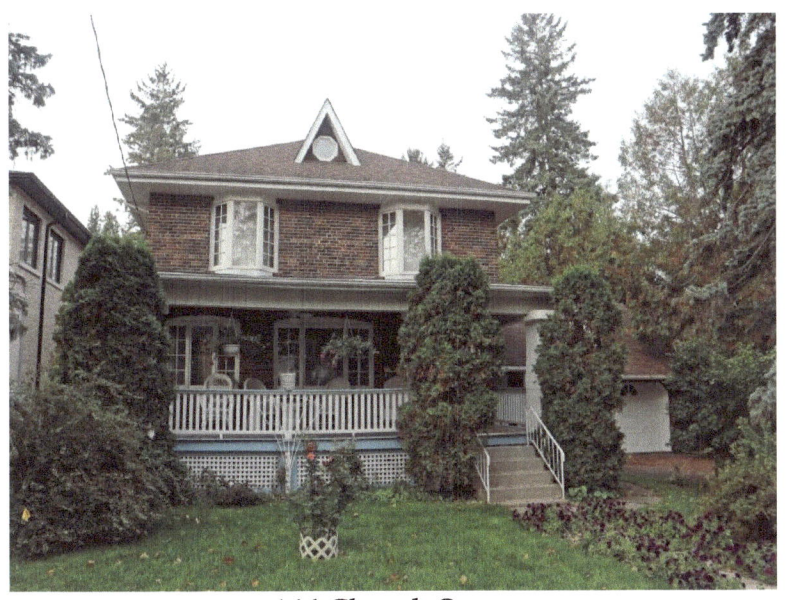

146 Church Street

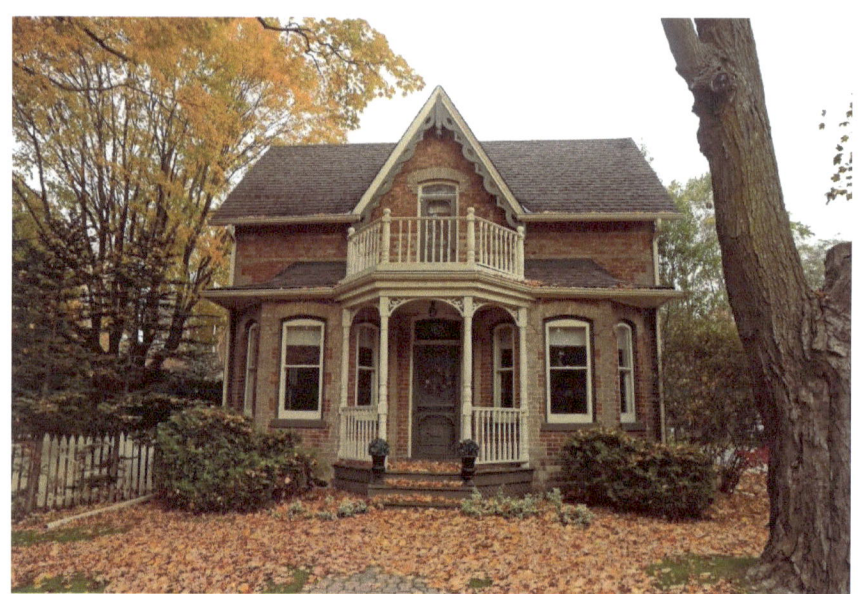

126 Frederick Street – Gothic Revival

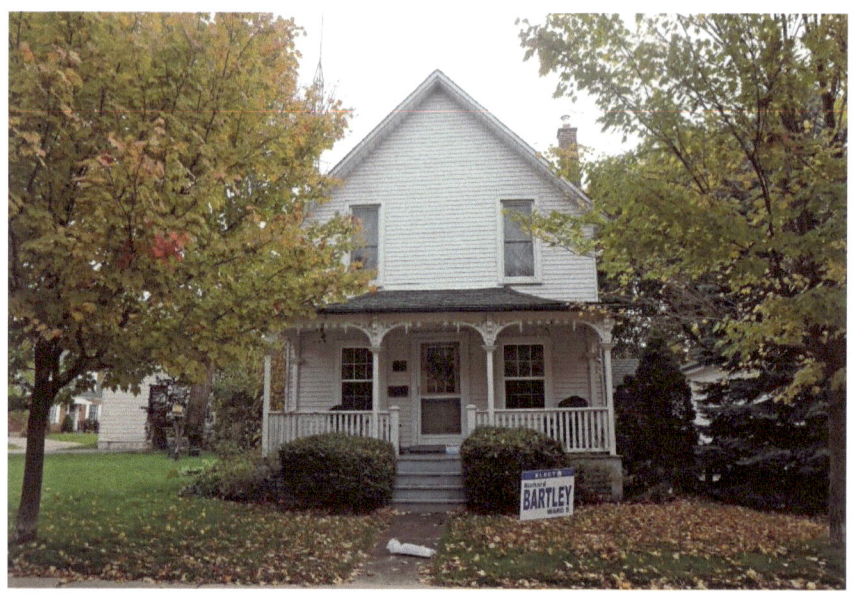

63 George Street – c. 1876 – Late Victorian Hybrid – built for Charles Perry, painter and decorator

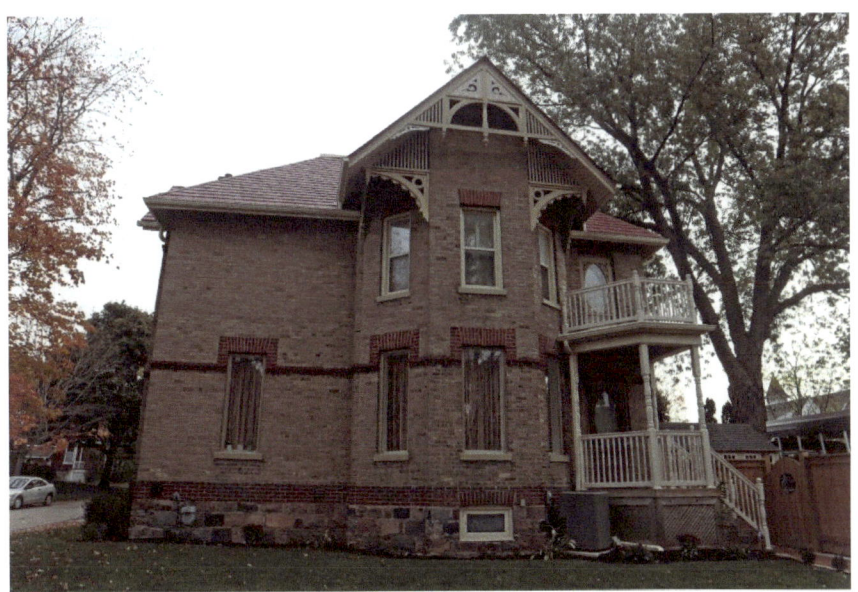

59 George Street – c. 1885 – Late Victorian Hybrid – built for brothers John and Thomas Casely – strong red brick banding around house, fretwork

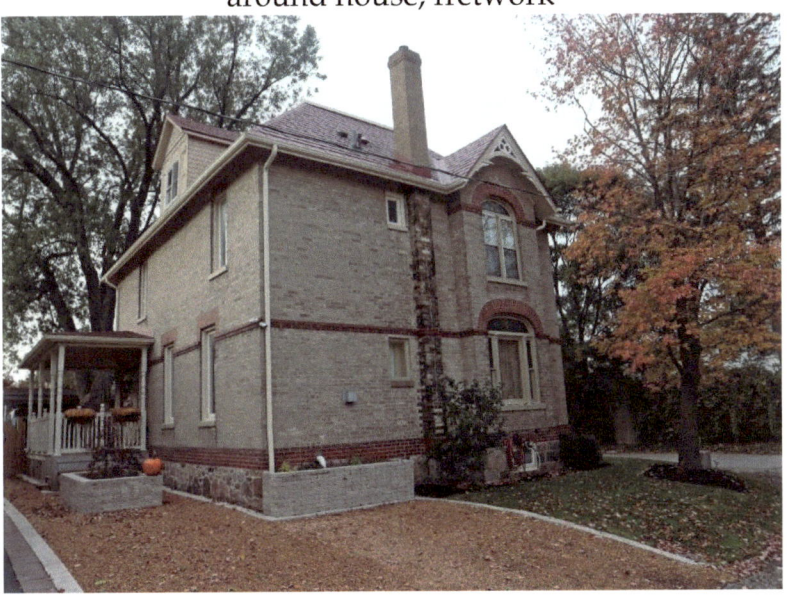

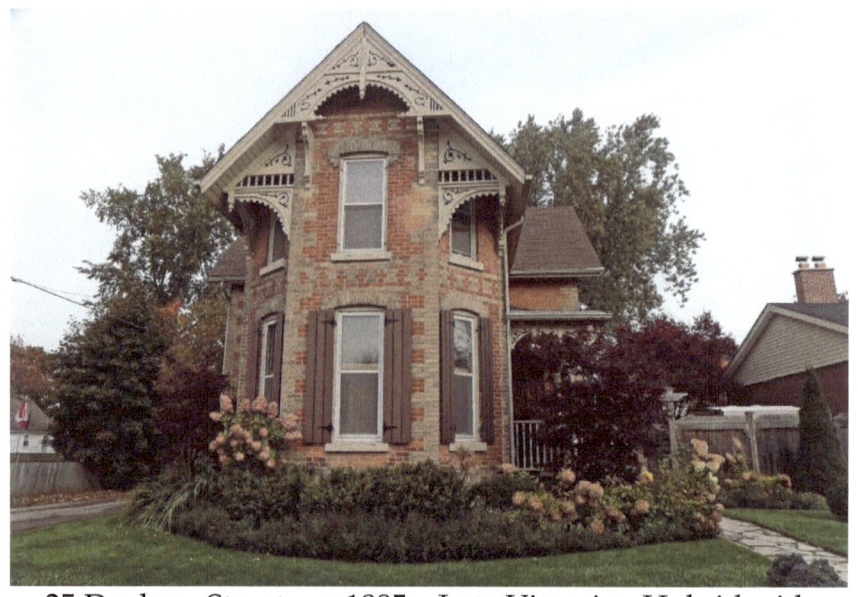

25 Duchess Street – c. 1885 – Late Victorian Hybrid with Queen Anne details – built for John and Thomas Casely - decorative brick, carved wooden fascia and porch, corner quoins, voussoirs, wooden post with capitals on ornately decorated porch for main entrance

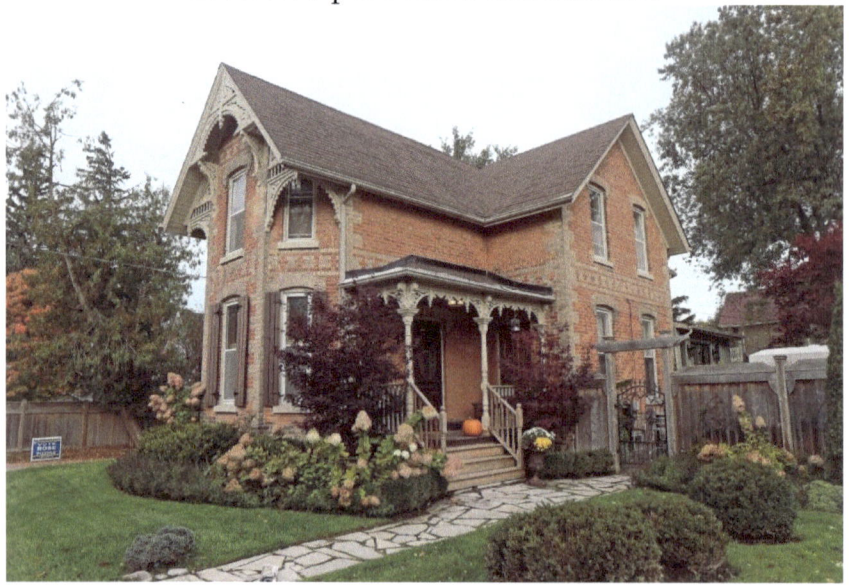

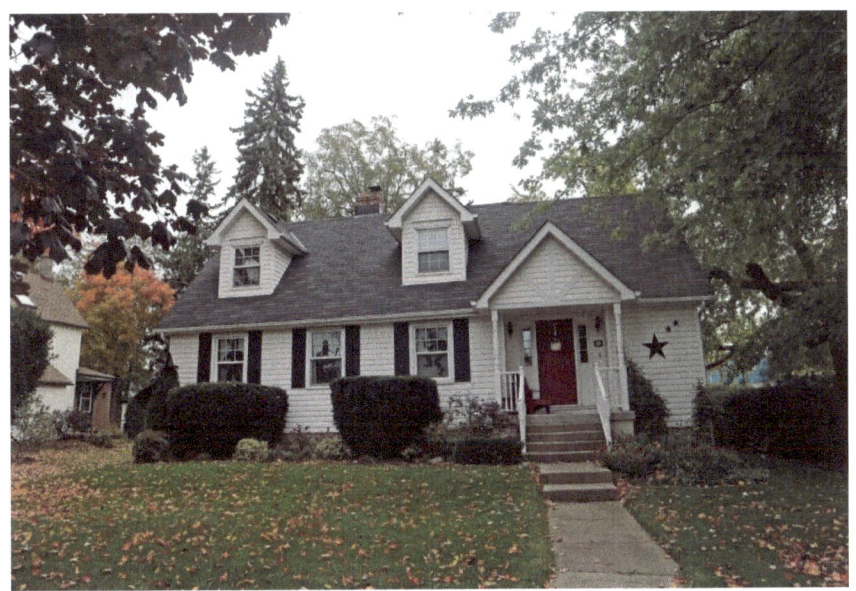

57 Victoria Street - dormers

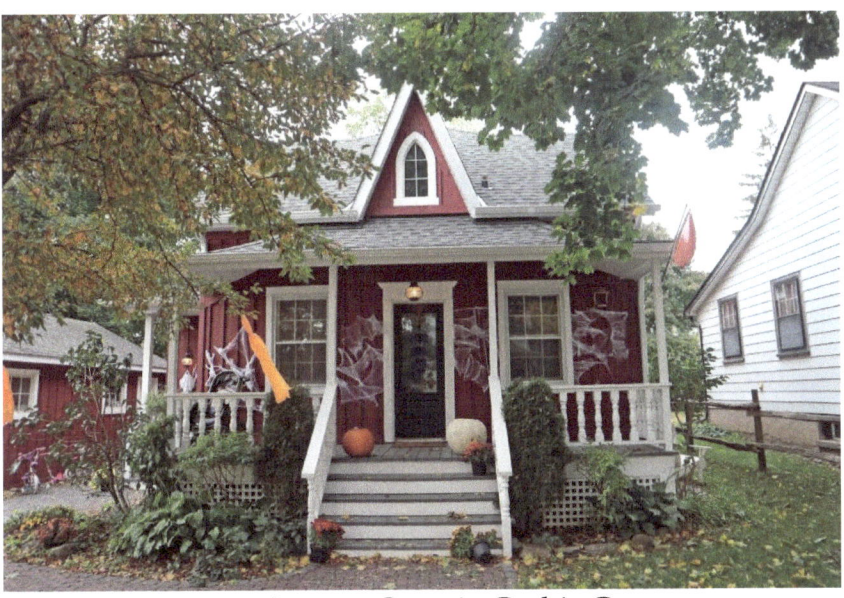

Victoria Street – Ontario Gothic Cottage

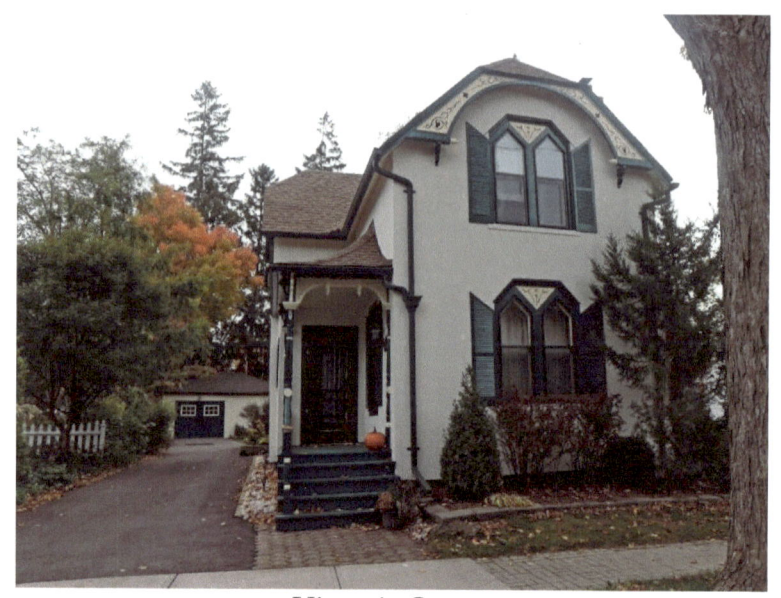
Victoria Street

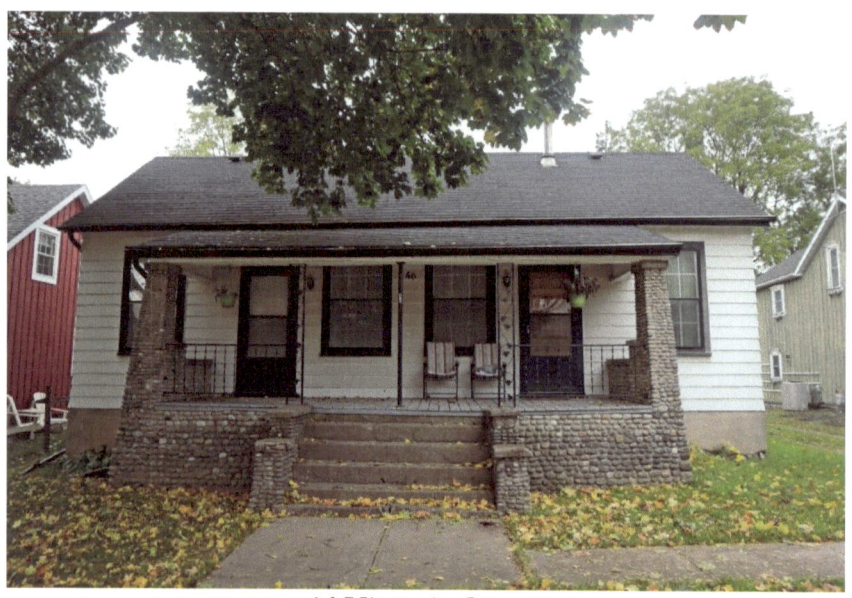
46 Victoria Street

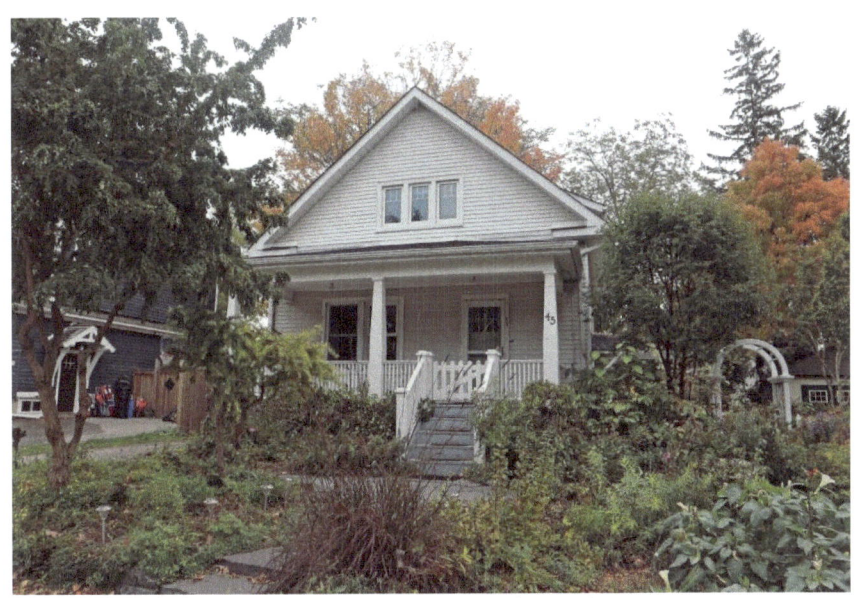

45 Victoria Street - Edwardian

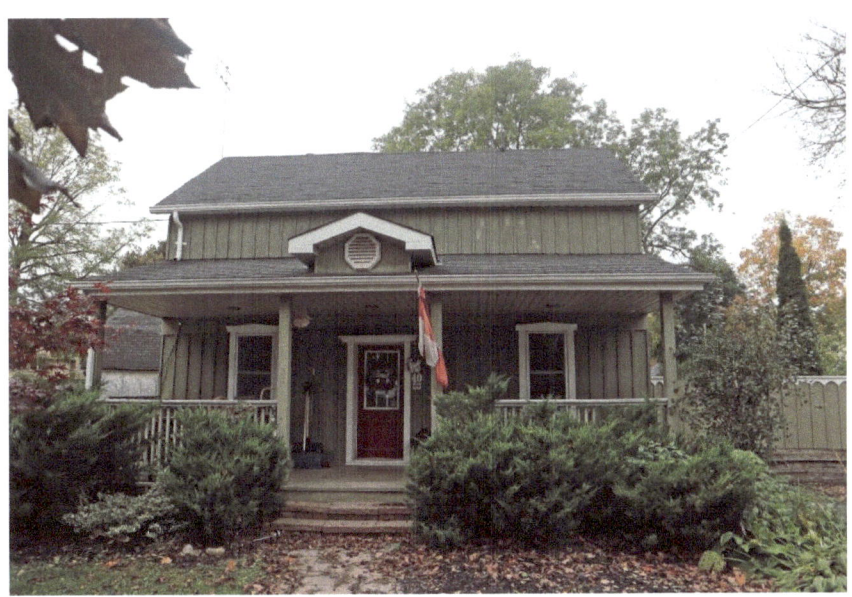

40 Victoria Street

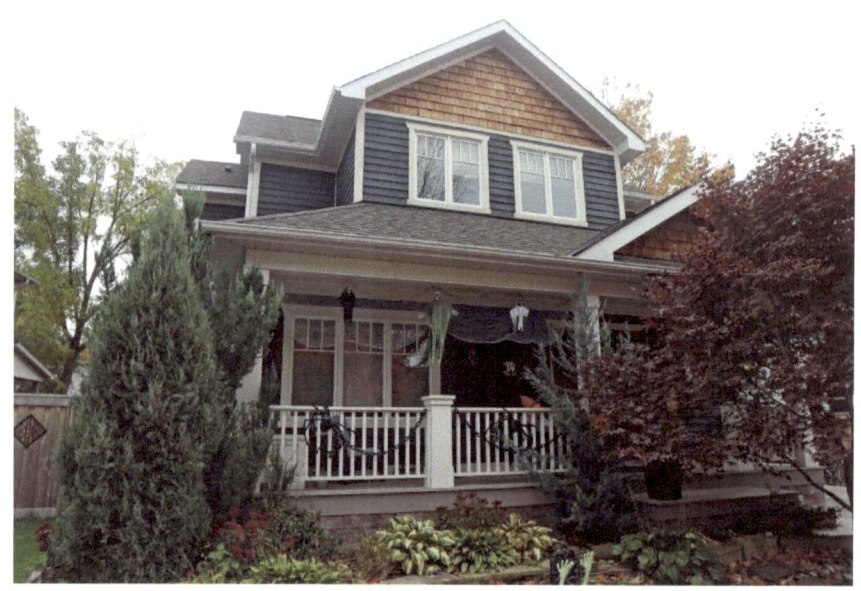

39 Victoria Street

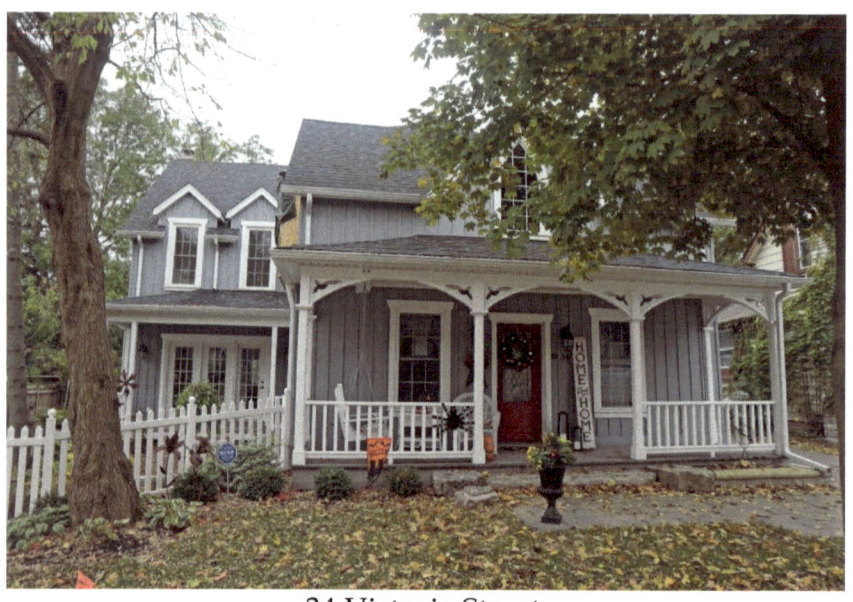

34 Victoria Street

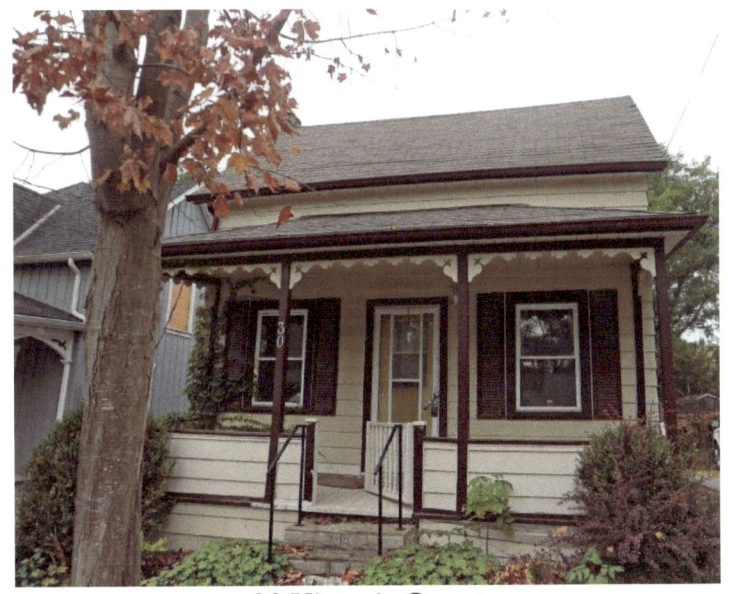

30 Victoria Street

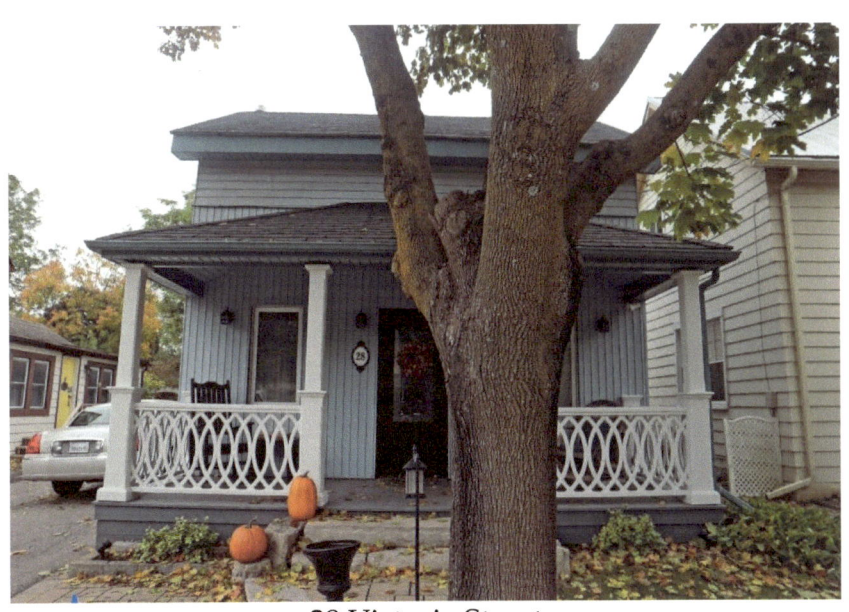

28 Victoria Street

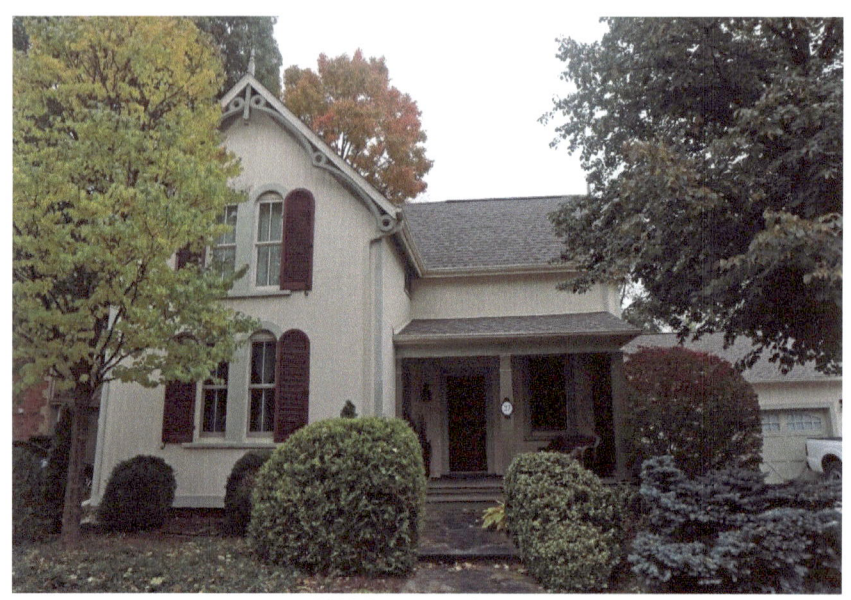

27 Victoria Street

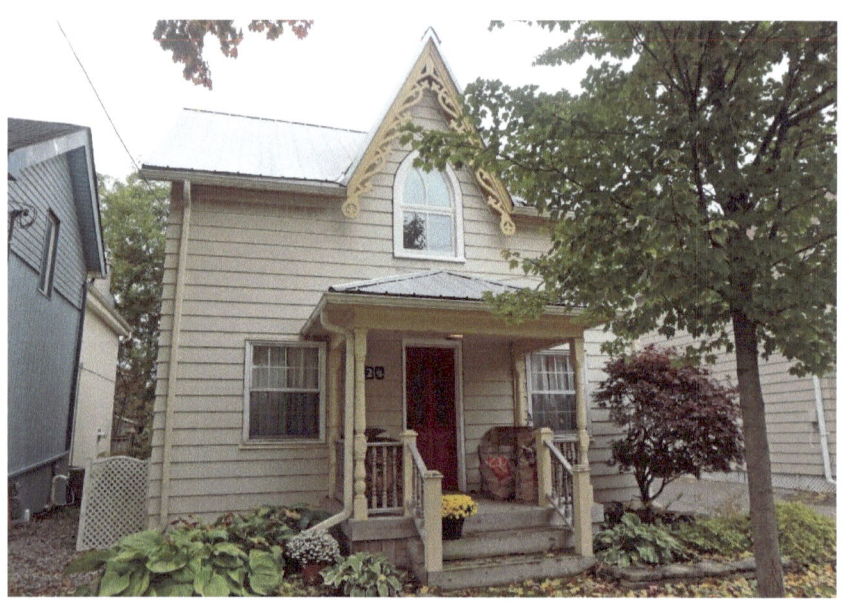

24 Victoria Street – Gothic Revival

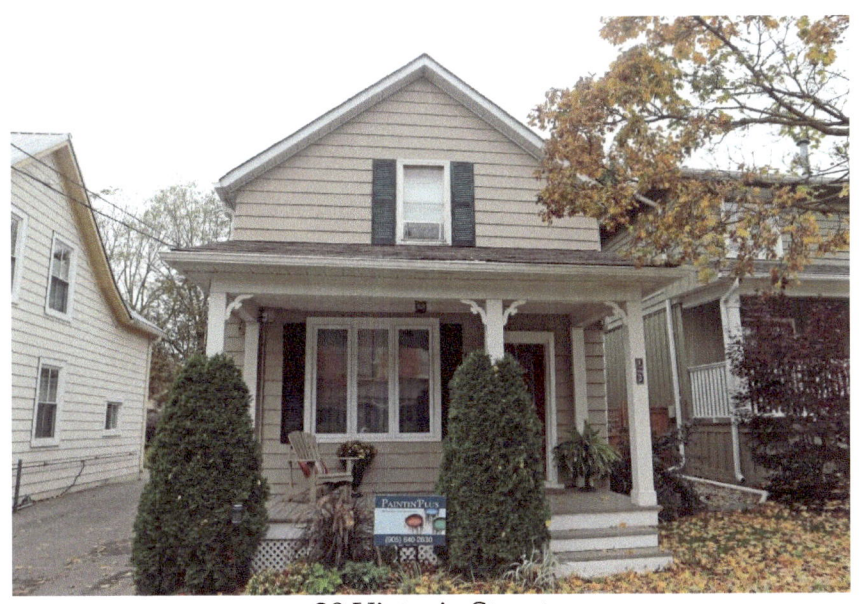
20 Victoria Street

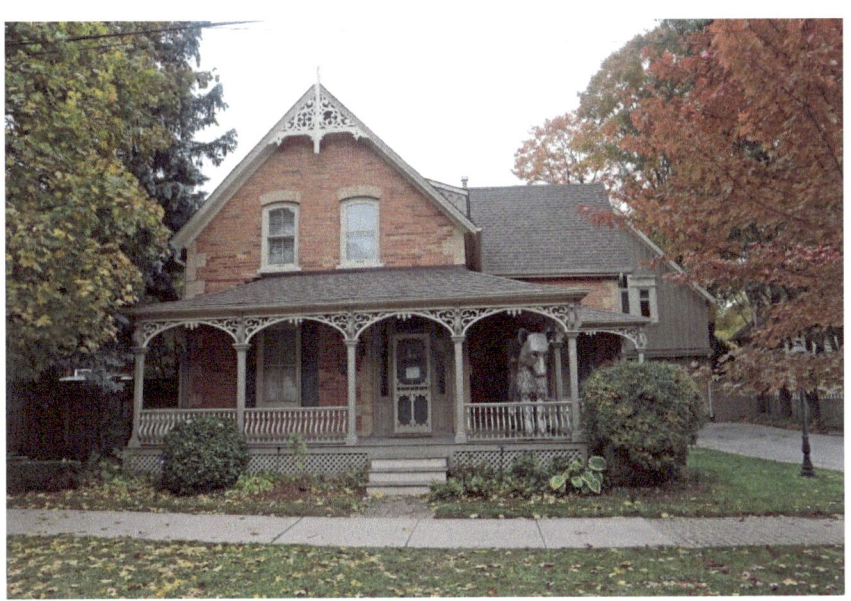
Victoria Street

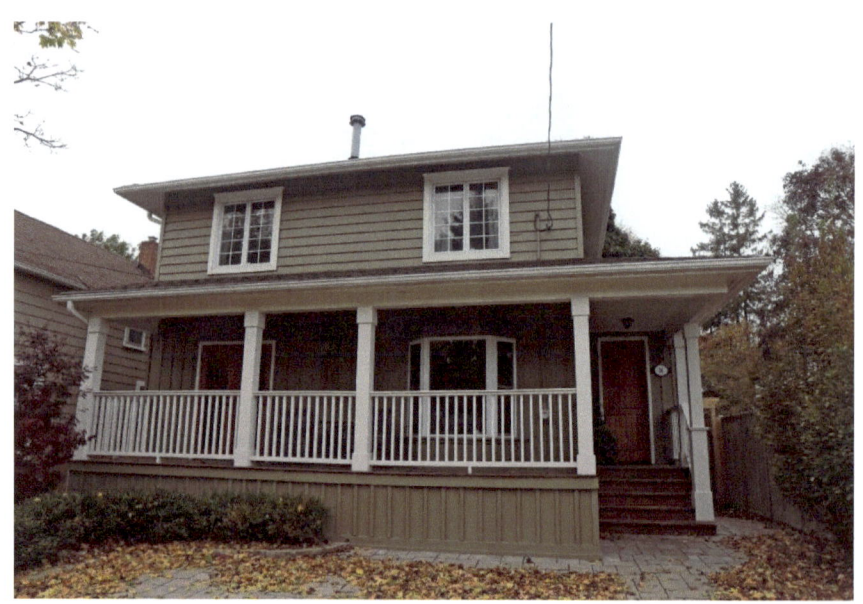

14 Victoria Street

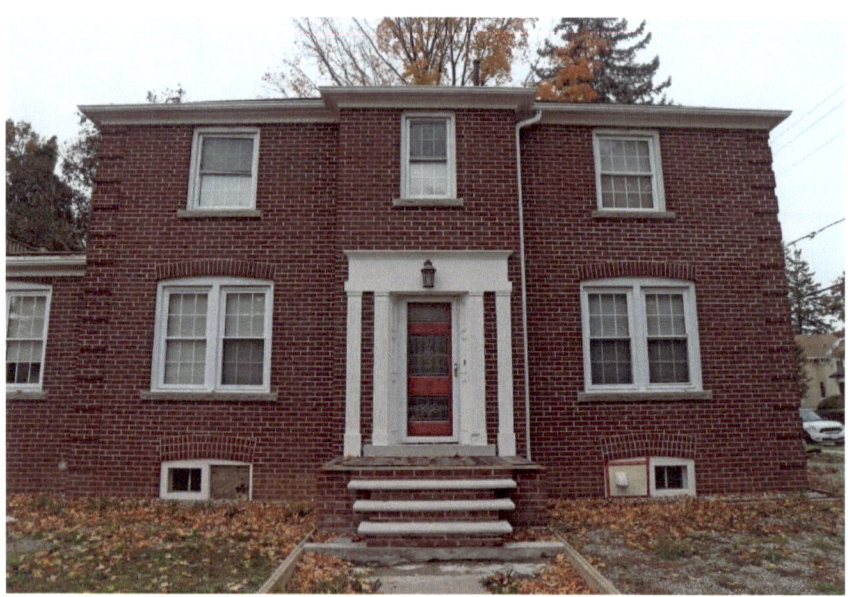

Victoria Street

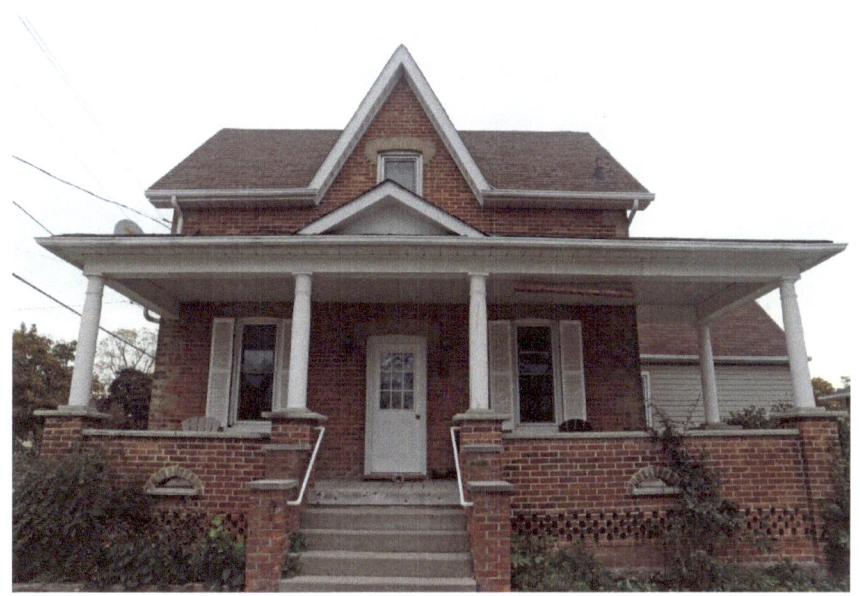

Clarke Street

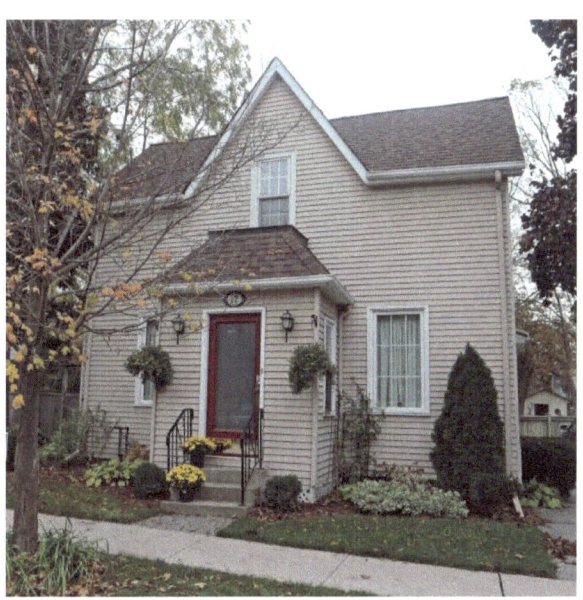

17 Clarke Street – c. 1889 – Gothic Revival – the home of 'Cobblestone Porch-Doctor' Jacob Jennings – known for making cobblestone porch additions

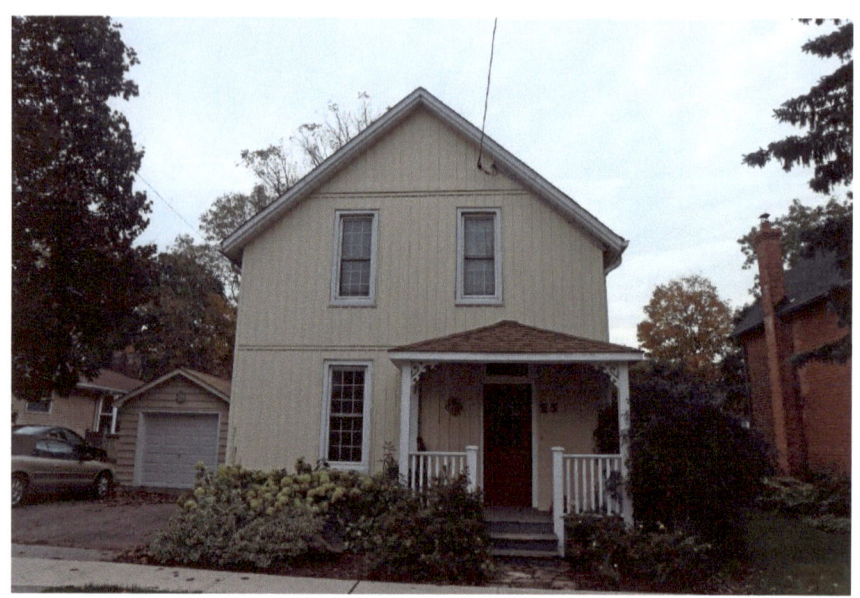

25 Clarke Street – c. 1889 – 1½ storey Vernacular – large farmhouse style – home of Elizabeth and Obediah Fleury, owner of Fleury Foundry which made tools for laborers – wood board and batten, string course, open porch

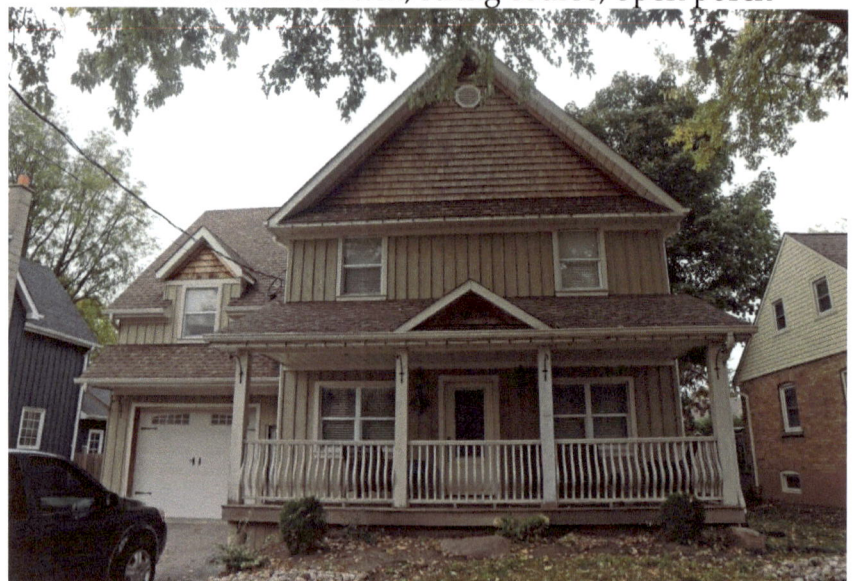

32 Clarke Street

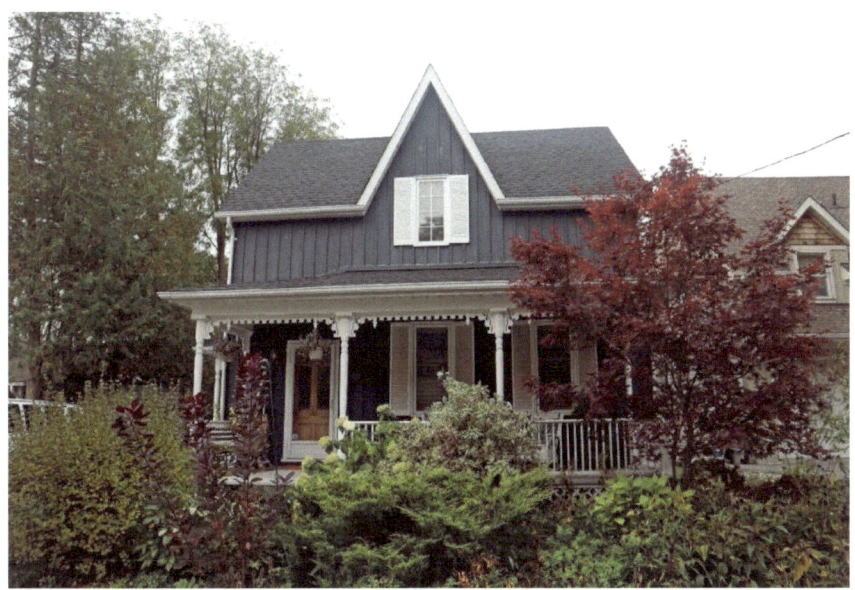

38 Clarke Street – c. 1889 – Gothic Revival Ontario Farmhouse – built for James Young, stone mason – open verandah

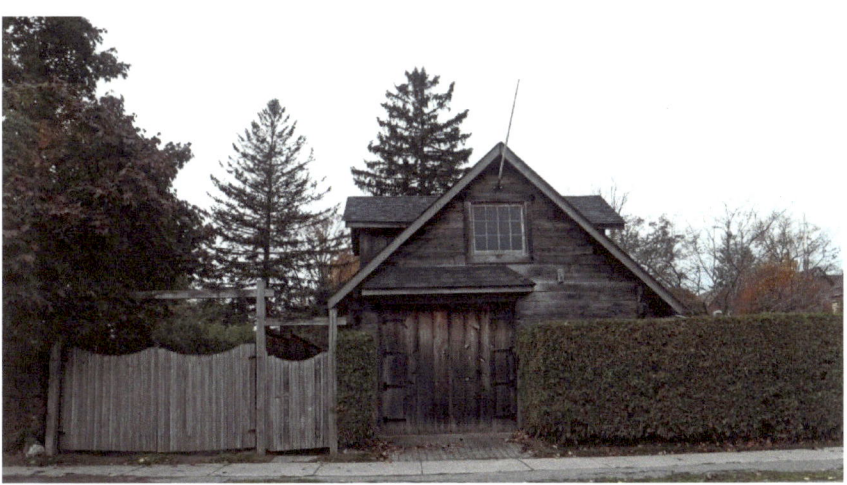

Clarke Street

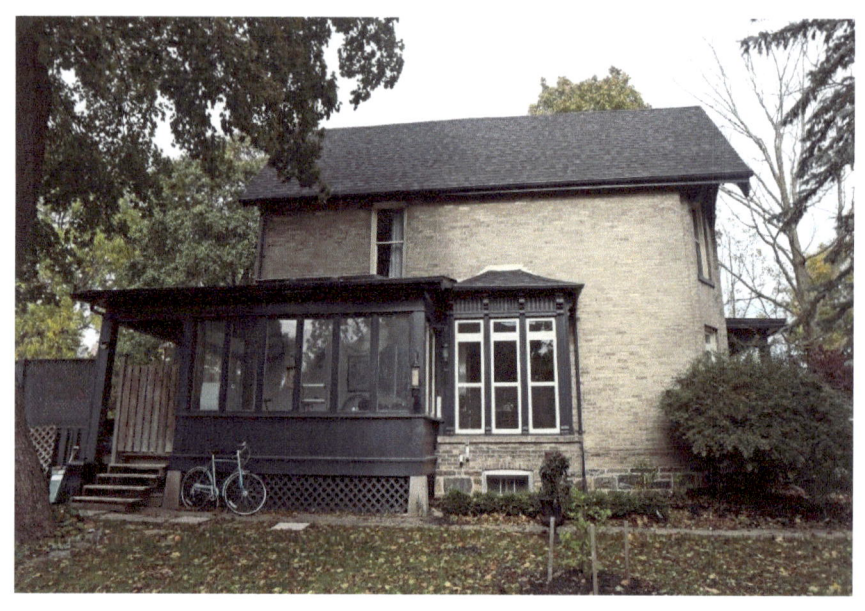

Somerville Street

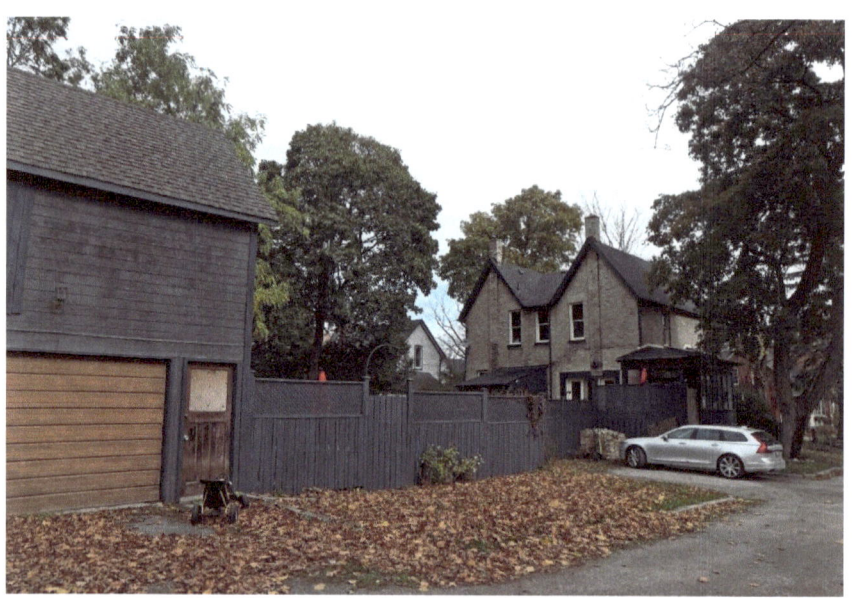

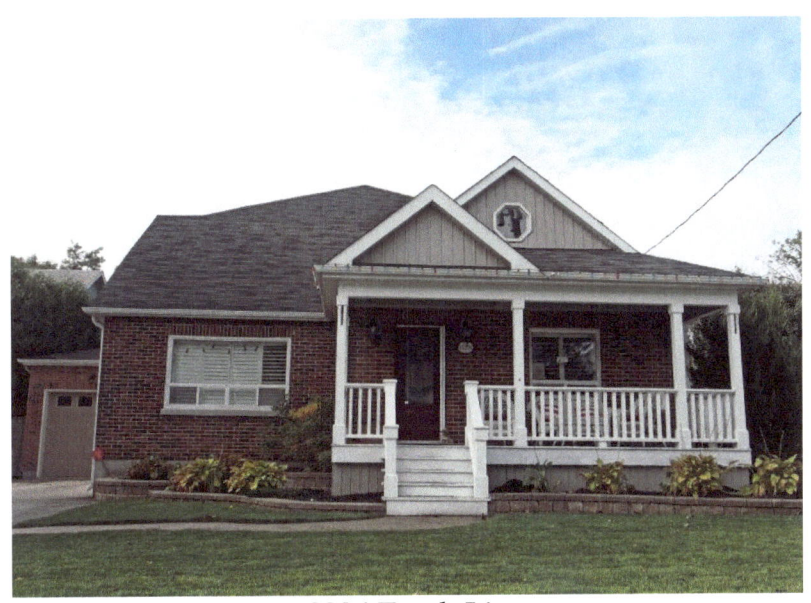

12226 Tenth Line

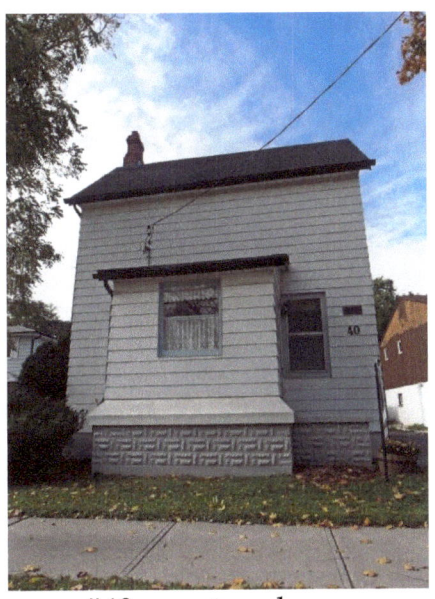

#40 – century home

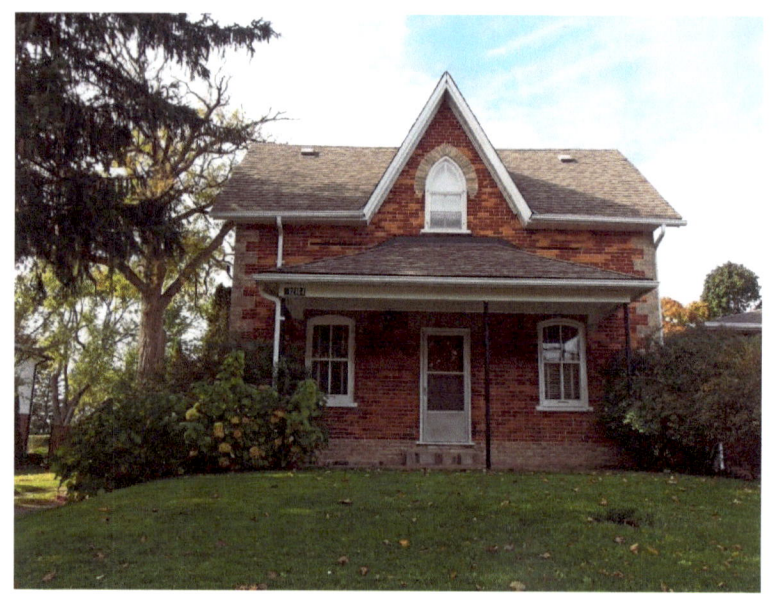

12164 Tenth Line – Gothic Revival

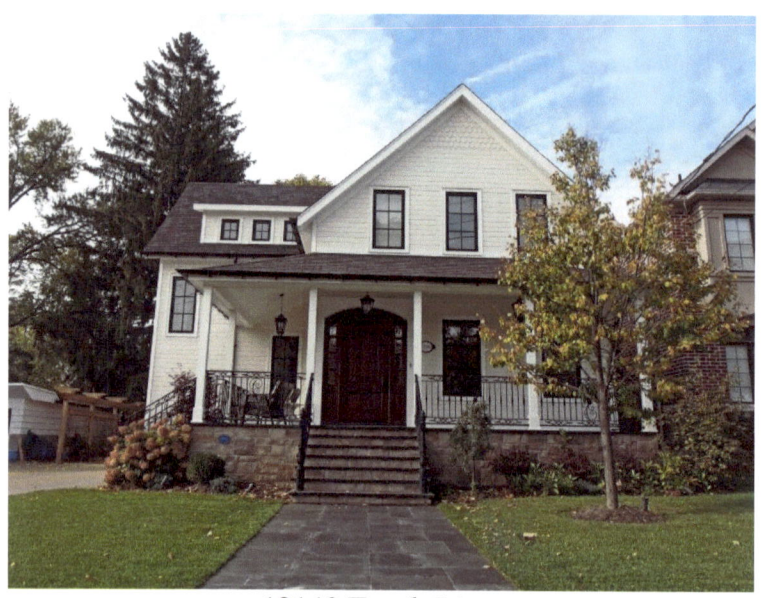

12140 Tenth Line

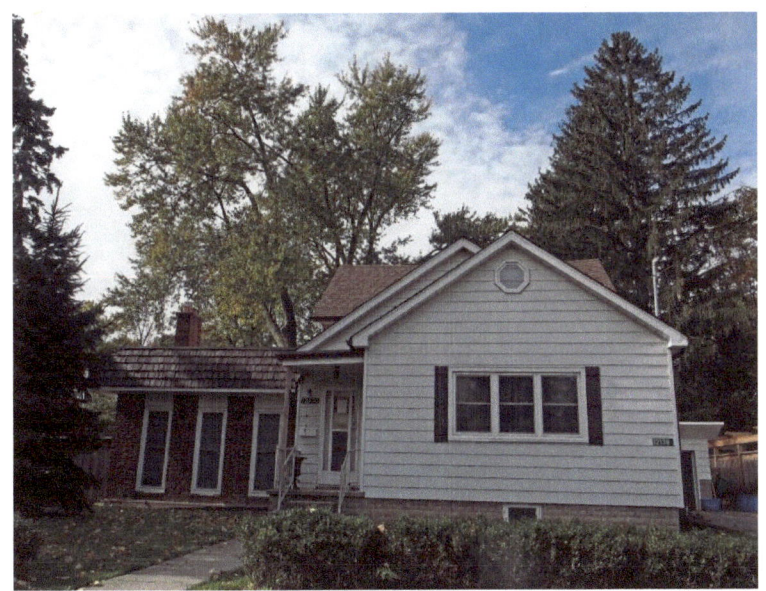

12130 Tenth Line

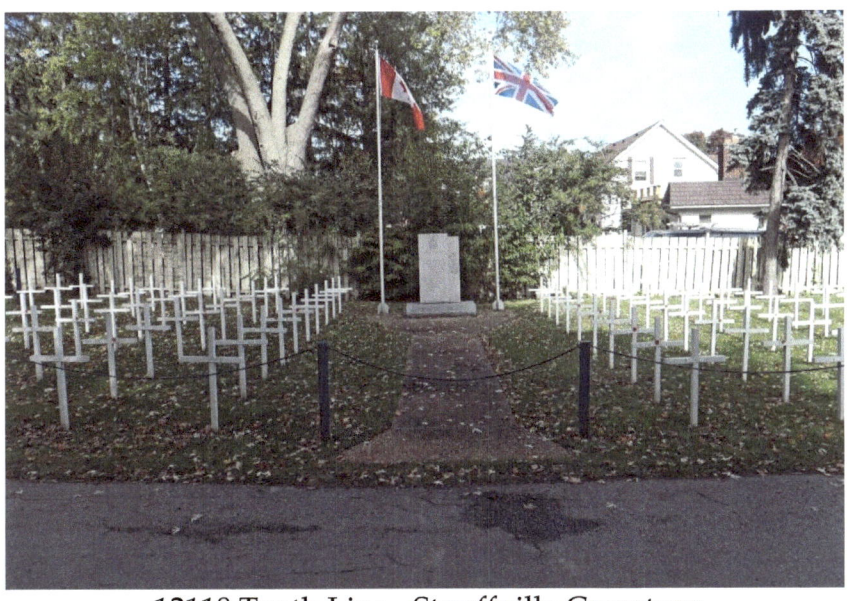

12118 Tenth Line - Stouffville Cemetery

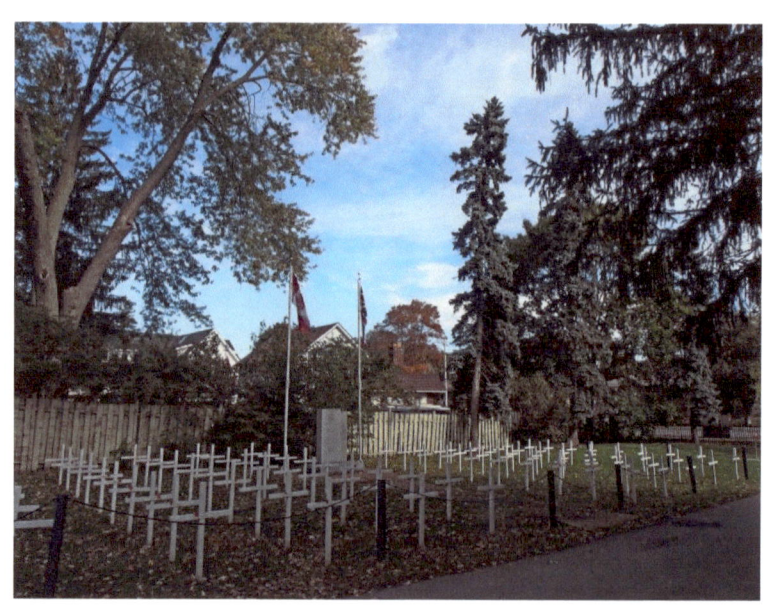

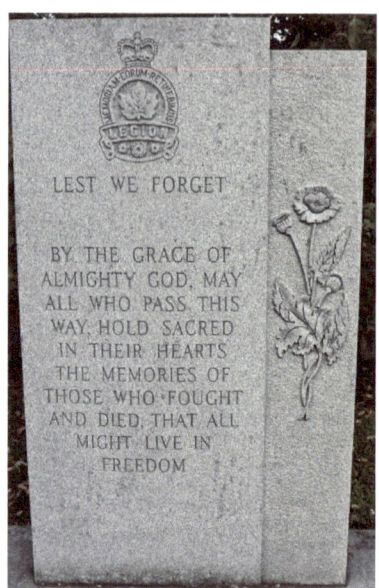

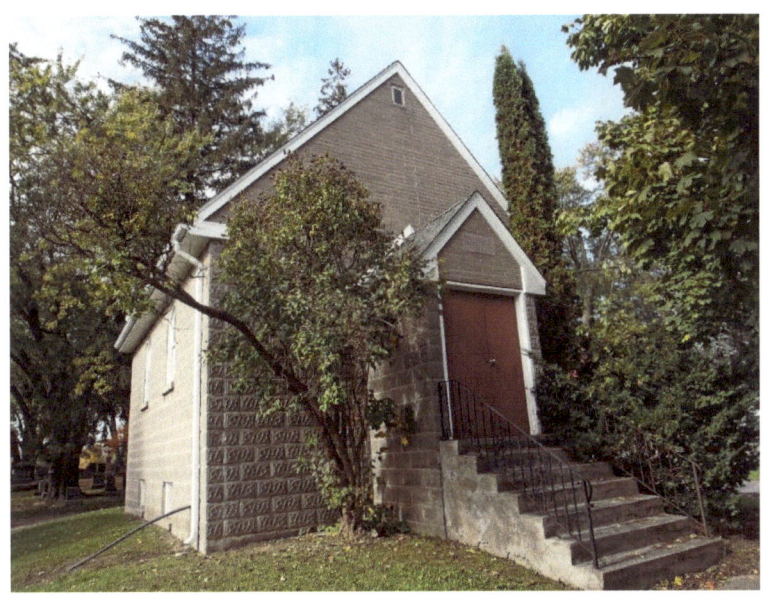

Thomas Williamson Memorial Chapel – 1952

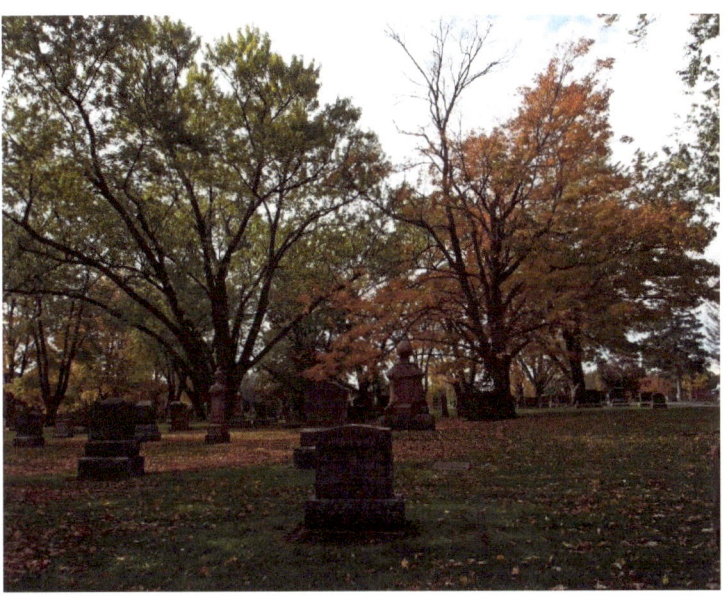

# Building Styles

**Georgian**, before 1860 – This style began with the British King Georges in the 18th century. These buildings have balanced facades around a central door, medium-pitched gable roofs, and small paned windows.

**Gothic Revival**, 1830-1890 – These decorative buildings have sharply-pitched gables with highly detailed verge boards, pointed-arch window openings, and dichromatic brickwork. It is a common style in Ontario.

**Italianate**, 1850-1900 – A two story rectangular building with a mild hip roof, a projecting frontispiece, and generous eaves with ornate cornice brackets was the basis of the style; often there are large sash windows, quoins, ornate detailing on the windows, belvederes and wraparound verandahs. Italianate commercial buildings often have cast iron cresting and elegant window surrounds.

**Neo-colonial** (also Colonial Revival, Georgian Revival or Neo-Georgian) architecture seeks to revive elements of architectural style of American colonial architecture of the period around the Revolutionary War which drew strongly from Georgian architecture of Great Britain. Architecture from the 18th and early 19th centuries in Ontario includes a wide assortment of detailing and ornament applied to a design centered around the fireplace and the source of water. Structures are typically two stories, have a symmetrical front facade with elaborate front doorways, often with decorative crown pediments, fanlights, and sidelights, symmetrical windows flanking the front entrance, often in pairs or threes, and columned porches.

**Ontario Cottage** - one or one-and-a-half story buildings with a cottage or hip roof. The cottage roof is an equal hip roof where each hip extends to a point in the center of the roof. The hip roof has a long hip in the center. The Ontario Cottage is the vernacular design of the Regency Cottage which generally has a more ornate doorway and a partial or full verandah surrounding it. The roof can have a dormer, a belvedere, and generally two chimneys.

**Queen Anne**, 1885-1900 – This style is distinguished by an irregular outline featuring a combination of an offset tower, broad gables, projecting two-storey bays, verandahs, multi-sloped roofs, and tall, decorative chimneys. A mixture of brick and wood is common. Windows often have one large single-paned bottom sash and small panes in the upper sash.

**Romanesque Revival**, 1880-1910 – This style hearkens back to medieval architecture of the 11th and 12th centuries with a heavy appearance, blocky towers and rounded arches.

**Vernacular/Traditional Mode** 1638 - 1950
Influenced but not defined by a particular style, vernacular buildings are made from easily available materials and exhibit local design characteristics.

**Victorian** - In Ontario, a Victorian style building can be seen as any building built between 1840 and 1900 that doesn't fit into any of the other categories. It encompasses a large group of buildings constructed in brick, stone, and timber, using an eclectic mixture of Classical and Gothic motifs.

# Other Books by Barbara Raue

Coins of Gold
Arrows, Indians and Love
The Life and Times of Barbara
The Cromwell Family Book
Laura Secord Discovered
Daddy Where Are You?

Montana Series
Book 1: Montana Dream
Book 2: Life on the Montana Frontier
Book 3: Montana to Boston and Back
Book 4: Montana Sons Go to War
Book 5: Montana Sons Return from War

Visit Barbara's website to view all of her books
http://barbararaue.ca

© 2018 by Barbara Raue - All the photos in this book have been taken with my cameras. I own the rights to them.

www.ingramcontent.com/pod-product-compliance
Lightning Source LLC
Chambersburg PA
CBHW040236220526
45473CB00001B/259